The Information Revolution

OPPOSING VIEWPOINTS®

D0107663

The Information Revolution

Opposing Viewpoints®

WITHDRAWN

Other Books of Related Interest

OPPOSING VIEWPOINTS SERIES

Censorship
The Internet
Mass Media
Technology and Society

CURRENT CONTROVERSIES SERIES

Censorship
Civil Liberties
Computers and Society
Free Speech
The Information Age
The Information Highway

AT ISSUE SERIES

Computers and Education
The Future of the Internet
Should There Be Limits to Free Speech?

The Information Revolution

OPPOSING VIEWPOINTS®

Laura K. Egendorf, *Book Editor*

Daniel Leone, *President*
Bonnie Szumski, *Publisher*
Scott Barbour, *Managing Editor*
Helen Cothran, *Senior Editor*

OPPOSING
VIEWPOINTS®
SERIES

GREENHAVEN
PRESS ®

THOMSON
———*———™
GALE

San Diego • Detroit • New York • San Francisco • Cleveland
New Haven, Conn. • Waterville, Maine • London • Munich

Cover credit: Photodisc

LIBRARY OF CONGRESS CATALOGING-IN-PUBLICATION DATA

The information revolution : opposing viewpoints / Laura K. Egendorf, book editor.
p. cm. — (Opposing viewpoints series)
Includes bibliographical references and index.
ISBN 0-7377-1694-0 (pbk. : alk. paper) — ISBN 0-7377-1693-2 (lib. : alk. paper)
1. Information technology—Social aspects. 2. Information society. I. Egendorf, Laura K., 1973–
T58.5.I526 2004
303.48'33—dc21
2003044813

Printed in the United States of America

"Congress shall make no law. . .abridging the freedom of speech, or of the press."

First Amendment to the U.S. Constitution

The basic foundation of our democracy is the First Amendment guarantee of freedom of expression. The Opposing Viewpoints Series is dedicated to the concept of this basic freedom and the idea that it is more important to practice it than to enshrine it.

Contents

Why Consider Opposing Viewpoints?   11

Introduction   14

Chapter 1: How Has the Internet Changed Society?

Chapter Preface   19

1. The Information Revolution Has Created a Digital Divide   21
   Larry Irving

2. The Information Revolution Has Not Created a Digital Divide   31
   Adam D. Thierer

3. The Internet Has Transformed the Economy   38
   Robert J. Eaton

4. The Internet Has Not Transformed the Economy   44
   Dwight R. Lee

5. The Internet Promotes Social Interaction   48
   William J. Mitchell

6. The Internet Discourages Social Interaction   57
   Andrew L. Shapiro

Periodical Bibliography   66

Chapter 2: Has the Information Revolution Improved Education?

Chapter Preface   68

1. Technology Has Improved Education   70
   Margaret Honey

2. Technology Alone Has Not Improved Education   78
   Andrew T. LeFevre

3. The Information Revolution Has Improved Off-Campus Education   83
   Kathleen B. Davey

4. The Information Revolution Has Not Improved Off-Campus Education   89
   Dave Wilson

5. Government-Sponsored Programs Have Made
   Computers Accessible to Poorer Schools   93
   William E. Kennard

6. Government-Sponsored Programs Are
   Unnecessary   98
   Adam D. Thierer

Periodical Bibliography   102

**Chapter 3: Are Rights Threatened in the
Information Age?**

Chapter Preface   104

1. New Technologies Are a Threat to Privacy   106
   Simson Garfinkel

2. New Technologies Are Not a Threat to Privacy   113
   Greg Miller

3. Restricting Obscenity on the Internet Threatens
   Free Speech   120
   Mike Godwin

4. Restricting Obscenity on the Internet Does Not
   Threaten Free Speech   126
   Theodore B. Olson

5. Intellectual Property Rights Require Greater
   Protection   134
   Bonnie J.K. Richardson

6. Intellectual Property Rights Do Not Require
   Greater Protection   141
   James Boyle

Periodical Bibliography   148

**Chapter 4: What Will Be the Future of the
Information Revolution?**

Chapter Preface   150

1. The Information Revolution Will Continue to
   Benefit Society   152
   Joseph F. Coates

2. The Information Revolution Will Not Be
   a Panacea   160
   Economist

3. The Information Revolution Will Benefit
   Developing Nations   165
   David Morrison

4. The Information Revolution Will Not Benefit
   Developing Nations   172
   Kunda Dixit

5. The Information Revolution Will Become More
   Competitive   177
   Nicholas Imparato

6. The Internet Could Help Build a Global
   Democracy   181
   Andrew Hammer

Periodical Bibliography   187

For Further Discussion   188
Organizations to Contact   190
Bibliography of Books   195
Index   197

Why Consider Opposing Viewpoints?

"The only way in which a human being can make some approach to knowing the whole of a subject is by hearing what can be said about it by persons of every variety of opinion and studying all modes in which it can be looked at by every character of mind. No wise man ever acquired his wisdom in any mode but this."

John Stuart Mill

In our media-intensive culture it is not difficult to find differing opinions. Thousands of newspapers and magazines and dozens of radio and television talk shows resound with differing points of view. The difficulty lies in deciding which opinion to agree with and which "experts" seem the most credible. The more inundated we become with differing opinions and claims, the more essential it is to hone critical reading and thinking skills to evaluate these ideas. Opposing Viewpoints books address this problem directly by presenting stimulating debates that can be used to enhance and teach these skills. The varied opinions contained in each book examine many different aspects of a single issue. While examining these conveniently edited opposing views, readers can develop critical thinking skills such as the ability to compare and contrast authors' credibility, facts, argumentation styles, use of persuasive techniques, and other stylistic tools. In short, the Opposing Viewpoints Series is an ideal way to attain the higher-level thinking and reading skills so essential in a culture of diverse and contradictory opinions.

In addition to providing a tool for critical thinking, Opposing Viewpoints books challenge readers to question their own strongly held opinions and assumptions. Most people form their opinions on the basis of upbringing, peer pressure, and personal, cultural, or professional bias. By reading carefully balanced opposing views, readers must directly confront new ideas as well as the opinions of those with whom they disagree. This is not to simplistically argue that everyone who reads opposing views will—or should—change his or her opinion. Instead, the series enhances readers' understanding of their own views by encouraging confrontation with opposing ideas. Careful examination of others' views can lead to the readers' understanding of the logical inconsistencies in their own opinions, perspective on why they hold an opinion, and the consideration of the possibility that their opinion requires further evaluation.

Evaluating Other Opinions

To ensure that this type of examination occurs, Opposing Viewpoints books present all types of opinions. Prominent spokespeople on different sides of each issue as well as well-known professionals from many disciplines challenge the reader. An additional goal of the series is to provide a forum for other, less known, or even unpopular viewpoints. The opinion of an ordinary person who has had to make the decision to cut off life support from a terminally ill relative, for example, may be just as valuable and provide just as much insight as a medical ethicist's professional opinion. The editors have two additional purposes in including these less known views. One, the editors encourage readers to respect others' opinions—even when not enhanced by professional credibility. It is only by reading or listening to and objectively evaluating others' ideas that one can determine whether they are worthy of consideration. Two, the inclusion of such viewpoints encourages the important critical thinking skill of objectively evaluating an author's credentials and bias. This evaluation will illuminate an author's reasons for taking a particular stance on an issue and will aid in readers' evaluation of the author's ideas.

It is our hope that these books will give readers a deeper understanding of the issues debated and an appreciation of the complexity of even seemingly simple issues when good and honest people disagree. This awareness is particularly important in a democratic society such as ours in which people enter into public debate to determine the common good. Those with whom one disagrees should not be regarded as enemies but rather as people whose views deserve careful examination and may shed light on one's own.

Thomas Jefferson once said that "difference of opinion leads to inquiry, and inquiry to truth." Jefferson, a broadly educated man, argued that "if a nation expects to be ignorant and free . . . it expects what never was and never will be." As individuals and as a nation, it is imperative that we consider the opinions of others and examine them with skill and discernment. The Opposing Viewpoints Series is intended to help readers achieve this goal.

David L. Bender and Bruno Leone,
Founders

Greenhaven Press anthologies primarily consist of previously published material taken from a variety of sources, including periodicals, books, scholarly journals, newspapers, government documents, and position papers from private and public organizations. These original sources are often edited for length and to ensure their accessibility for a young adult audience. The anthology editors also change the original titles of these works in order to clearly present the main thesis of each viewpoint and to explicitly indicate the opinion presented in the viewpoint. These alterations are made in consideration of both the reading and comprehension levels of a young adult audience. Every effort is made to ensure that Greenhaven Press accurately reflects the original intent of the authors included in this anthology.

Introduction

"The much-heralded information superhighway . . . [is] a development in technology so remarkable in scope that it could equal the telephone or the steam engine in its ability to . . . improve our quality of life."
—Rick Boucher, U.S. representative from Virginia

Humans have always looked toward the future. People involved in the science and technology industries continually make predictions, and quite often their forecasts are no more accurate than what past civilizations gleaned by looking at tea leaves. Despite the visions depicted in exhibits at World's Fairs, no one is living in outer space à la the Jetsons. On the other hand, IBM founder Thomas J. Watson turned out to be laughably wrong for proclaiming in 1941, "I think there is a world market for about five computers." With today's computer market millions of times larger than Watson ever envisioned, visionaries have continued to make predictions as to how computers and the Internet will change society, especially in two fields that affect nearly everyone: education and business.

In January 1991 Senator Al Gore wrote in the *Futurist* that students would have access to devices that would give them "access to digital libraries and information that can expand their knowledge and awareness of the world around them." Richard W. Riley, the secretary of education for the Clinton administration, wrote in the winter 1995 edition of *Issues in Science and Technology*: "It is in the schools that the United States will obtain the greatest returns in its investments in technology—immediate returns in the forms of more productive and rewarding teaching and learning."

Similar predictions were made concerning computers' impact on business. In a 1994 article in *National Forum*, Virginia congressman Rick Boucher forecast ways in which the Internet would change business and industry. He asserted that companies would be able to transmit sales orders, contracts, and business plans across the country "without the loss of time, money, and clarity that hinders so much business communication." He also argued that the Information Revolution would reshape the economy. The dot-com explosion of the mid- to late-1990s brought with it another set of predictions, as market research firms, information technology analysts, and corporate honchos hypothesized skyrocketing profits for all Internet-based businesses. A 1996 study by two Columbia University professors predicted that the Internet would help the economy expand, "barring a crisis."

Not all of these predictions have come true. In reality, the effects of the Information Revolution on education and business have been a mixed bag. For example, reports by the National Education Association conclude that the Internet has transformed the U.S. educational system. According to a June 2001 NEA paper, Internet access in schools increased from 35 percent in 1994 to 95 percent in 1999. The association reports that students who use cutting-edge technology get better grades and turn in more creative work. However, several roadblocks have stymied the Internet's positive effects on education. Many teachers lack the knowledge and skills to successfully integrate technology into their daily lesson plans. Furthermore, the NEA states, "While 74 percent of classrooms in low-poverty schools are connected to the Internet, only 39 percent of classrooms in high-poverty schools have Internet access." The digital divide—the discrepancy between those who have access to computers and the Internet and those who do not—also affects children at home. While many students can come home and access digital libraries and archives as Gore predicted, others are not so fortunate. According to the National Telecommunications and Information Administration report *Falling Through the Net*, families that earn more than thirty-five thousand dollars are six times more likely than families below that income threshold to have Internet access.

Not only is access to information uneven, but the information itself is not always accurate or useful. The NEA cited a study by a Southern Colorado University professor who found that only 27 percent of the websites used by middle and high-school students for research provided reliable information. Overall, the Information Revolution's effects on education have been both good and bad. While computers have greatly improved the quality of education for some students, millions of children do not have full access to the benefits of modern technology, putting them at a distinct disadvantage.

The effects of computers and the Internet on business have been both good and bad as well. As for the purported Internet boom, it has turned out to be less-than-permanent. Although the Columbia University study determined that the Internet had added 200 billion dollars to the American economy, businesses that seemed like a sure bet in the heyday of the dot-com boom eventually became a collection of empty buildings. Because so many people had invested in these companies, the stock market tumbled; between March and April 2000, the NASDAQ stock exchange, which is dominated by technology stocks, lost one-third of its value. More than 140,000 dot-com employees lost their jobs in 2000 and 2001.

Nonetheless, in the long run, the failure of the dot-coms may benefit businesses that seek to maintain and develop an online presence because these companies are now more likely to formulate viable business plans and not offer their stocks at grossly inflated prices. As Paul Saffo, director of the Institute for the Future, explains in *Newsweek*, the dot-com failure "is the safety valve, the destructive renewing force that fires up people, ideas and capital and recombines them, creating new revolutions." The dot-coms were not a total failure, either—according to *Business Week*, at least one-fourth of publicly held Internet companies made a profit. *Business Week*'s analysis also sums up the overall impact information technology has had on the economy. The everyday lives of millions of people have been made more convenient—for example, through such advances as online purchasing—but the significant loss of jobs that occurred in 2000 and 2001 suggests that relying on the Internet to support the economy can have troubling consequences.

For better or ill, more than a half billion people are now connected to the Internet. While the Information Revolution may not fulfill all of the predictions made on its behalf, it has allowed students, consumers, and business executives around the world to share ideas without ever meeting in person and retrieve information that had been inaccessible barely a decade earlier. In *Opposing Viewpoints: The Information Revolution*, the authors debate the effects of computers and the Internet in the following chapters: How Has the Internet Changed Society? How Has the Information Revolution Improved Education? Are Rights Threatened in the Information Age? What Will Be the Future of the Information Revolution? In these chapters, the authors consider both the present and future of the Information Revolution.

CHAPTER 1

How Has the Internet Changed Society?

Chapter Preface

One of the greatest benefits of the Internet is that it enables people who share common interests, but who would never have met because they live in different parts of the world, to meet online and exchange ideas and opinions. However, the same technology that makes these exchanges possible has also made it easier for people with racist or other hateful views to disseminate their beliefs. As the rise of bigoted websites demonstrates, the impact that the Internet has had on society is not completely positive.

Among the more prominent of these sites are Stormfront (founded by former Ku Klux Klan leader Don Black in 1995), National Alliance (a white supremacist organization founded by the late William Pierce), and the website of the World Church of the Creator (WCOTC). According to the Anti-Defamation League's report "Hate on the World Wide Web: A Brief Guide to Cyberspace Bigotry," common features of these sites include anti-Semitic radio broadcasts, twisted interpretations of the Bible, and writings that level false accusations at Jews and African Americans. Stormfront and WCOTC also include "kids' pages," which offer puzzles and games for children's entertainment.

These websites, and numerous others that espouse similar opinions, have exploded throughout the United States because, as Stacia Brown points out in an article for the magazine *Sojourners*, "Online bigots enjoy full protection under the First Amendment and have access to a potentially limitless audience. Webmasters are anonymous and difficult to silence." While censorship might be considered an acceptable solution to the proliferation of hate-filled websites, neither the Anti-Defamation League nor other organizations that work to fight discrimination believe that hate speech should be restricted. According to the ADL: "The best way to combat hateful speech is with more speech." However, some Internet service providers (ISPs), such as America Online, have written anti-hate speech clauses into their service contracts; websites that violate these rules are pulled. Yahoo! has removed dozens of "clubs" that were sponsored by hate groups. In addition, the ADL has also developed the program HateFilter, which, once installed by parents, redirects users to an ADL page on hate groups if they attempt to visit some of the more offensive websites.

While these actions might slow the spread of hateful websites, it is unlikely that the Internet will ever be completely rid of intolerance. However, the negative consequences of the Internet should not lead people to discount the many ways the Information Revolution has improved society. In the following chapter, the authors debate the ways in which the Internet has changed the world.

"The chief concern with respect to household computer and Internet access is the growing digital divide."

The Information Revolution Has Created a Digital Divide

Larry Irving

In the following viewpoint, Larry Irving asserts that the Information Revolution has led to a digital divide—the divide between those who have access to computers and the Internet and those who do not. Irving contends that although the overall number of Americans with computers and Internet access has increased, the gap between people who have access to these technologies and those who do not continues to grow. According to Irving, minorities, rural households, low-income families, and senior citizens are significantly less likely than their white, younger, and urban counterparts to use electronic services. He concludes that the digital divide will continue to grow unless the government implements policies designed to improve access to all Americans. Irving is assistant secretary for communications, and information administrator for the National Telecommunications and Information Administration (NTIA). The NTIA is an agency of the U.S. Department of Commerce that works to encourage innovation and improve the quality and variety of telecommunications products and services.

As you read, consider the following questions:
1. What percentage of American households owned a personal computer in 1999?
2. Which urban areas have the lowest rate of electronic access?

Larry Irving, *Falling Through the Net: Defining the Digital Divide*, National Telecommunications and Information Administration.

The National Telecommunications and Information Administration (NTIA) is pleased to release *Falling Through the Net: Defining the Digital Divide.* This is our third report examining which American households have access to telephones, computers, and the Internet, and which do not. The "digital divide"—the divide between those with access to new technologies and those without—is now one of America's leading economic and civil rights issues. This report will help clarify which Americans are falling further behind, so that we can take concrete steps to redress this gap.

Overall, we have found that the number of Americans connected to the nation's information infrastructure is soaring. Nevertheless, this . . . report finds that a digital divide still exists, and, in many cases, is actually widening over time. Minorities, low-income persons, the less educated, and children of single-parent households, particularly when they reside in rural areas or central cities, are among the groups that lack access to information resources. . . .

While telephone penetration has remained stable across the nation, significant changes have occurred for personal computer ownership and Internet access. For the latter two categories, household rates have soared since 1994 for all demographic groups in all locations. These increases indicate that Americans across the board are increasingly embracing electronic services by employing them in their homes.

Despite increasing connectivity for all groups, in some areas the digital divide still exists and, in a number of cases, is growing. Some groups (such as certain minority or low-income households in rural America) still have personal computer (PC) and Internet penetration rates in the single digits. By contrast, other groups (such as higher-income, highly educated, or dual-parent households) have rising connectivity rates. One promising sign of change is that the gap between races for PC ownership has narrowed significantly at the highest income level (above $75,000).

Expanding Access to Electronic Services

Americans of every demographic group and geographic area have experienced a significant increase in computer ownership and Internet access. Nationwide, PC ownership is now at 42.1%, up from 24.1% in 1994 and 36.6% in 1997 (an increase of 74.7% and 15.0%, respectively). Households across rural, central city, and urban areas now own home computers in greater numbers; each area experienced at least a sixteen percentage point increase since 1994, and at least a five percentage point increase since 1997. Similarly, households of all ethnic groups, income levels, education levels, and ages have experienced a significant increase. Black and Hispanic households, for example, are now twice as likely to own PCs as they were in 1994. Internet access has also grown significantly in the last year: 26.2% of U.S. households now have Internet access, up from 18.6% in 1997 (an increase of 40.9%).

As with computer ownership, Internet access has increased for all demographic groups in all locations. In [1998] alone, for example, Internet access increased 40.5% for White households, 45.4% for Black households, and 44.8% for Hispanic households.

Disparities in Access

Despite these gains across American households, distinct disparities in access remain. Americans living in rural areas are less likely to be connected by PCs or the Internet—even when holding income constant. Indeed, at most income brackets below $35,000, those living in urban areas are at least 25% more likely to have Internet access than those in rural areas. Additionally, groups that already have low penetration rates (such as low-income, young, or certain minority households) are the least connected in rural areas and central cities.

The following demographic and geographic breakdowns are significant determinants of a household's likelihood of owning a computer or accessing the Internet from home:

Income. PC and Internet penetration rates both increase with higher income levels. Households at higher income levels are far more likely to own computers and access the Internet than those at the lowest income levels. Those with an income over $75,000 are more than five times as likely to have a computer at home and are more than seven times as likely to have home Internet access as those with an income under $10,000. Low income households in rural areas are the least connected, experiencing connectivity rates in the single digits for both PCs and Internet access. The contrast between low income households (earning between $5,000 and $9,999) in rural America and high income households (earning more than $75,000) in urban areas is particularly acute: 8.1% versus 76.5% for computer ownership, and 2.9% versus 62.0% for Internet access.

Internet Use by Race/Ethnicity

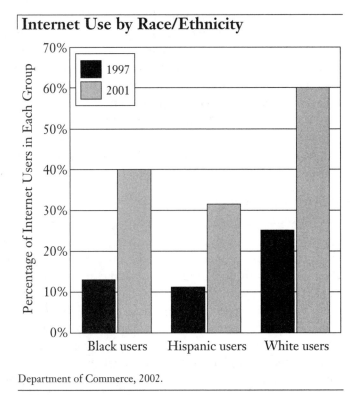

Department of Commerce, 2002.

The impact of income on Internet access is evident even among families with the same race and family structure. Among similarly-situated families (two parents, same race), a family earning more than $35,000 is two to almost six times as likely to have Internet access as a family earning less than $35,000. The most significant disparity is among Hispanic families: two-parent households earning more than $35,000 are nearly six times as likely to have Internet access as those earning less than $35,000.

Race/Origin. As with telephone penetration, race also influences connectivity. Unlike telephone penetration, however, households of Asian/Pacific Island descent have the clear lead in computer penetration (55.0%) and Internet access rates (36.0%), followed by White households (46.6% and 29.8%, respectively). Black and Hispanic households have far lower PC penetration levels (at 23.2% and 25.5%), and Internet access levels (11.2% and 12.6%). Again, geography and income influence these trends. Urban Asians/Pacific Islanders have the highest computer penetration rates (55.6%) and Internet access rates (36.5%). By contrast, rural Black households are the least connected group in terms of PC ownership (17.9%) or Internet access (7.1%). Black households earning less than $15,000 are also at the opposite end of the spectrum from high income Asians/Pacific Islanders for PC ownership (6.6% versus 85.0%).

The role of race or ethnic origin is highlighted when looking at similarly-situated families. A White, two-parent household earning less than $35,000 is nearly three times as likely to have Internet access as a comparable Black household and nearly four times as likely to have Internet access as Hispanic households in the same income category.

The Influence of Schools and Families

Education. Access to information resources is closely tied to one's level of education. Households at higher education levels are far more likely to own computers and access the Internet than those at the lowest education levels. Those with a college degree or higher are more than eight times as likely to have a computer at home (68.7% versus 7.9%) and are nearly sixteen times as likely to have home Internet access (48.9% versus 3.1%) as those with an elementary school education. In rural areas, the disparity is even greater. Those with a college degree or higher are more than eleven times as likely to have a computer at home (6.3% versus 69.7%) and are more than twenty-six times as likely to have home Internet access (1.8% versus 47.0%) as those with an elementary school education.

Household Type. As with telephones, the makeup of the household influences the likelihood of the household's access to electronic services. Computer ownership lags among single-parent households, especially female-headed households (31.7%), compared to married couples with children (61.8%). The same is true for Internet access (15.0% for female-headed households, 39.3% for dual-parent households).

When holding race constant, it is clear that family composition can still have a significant impact on Internet access. Overall, dual-parent White families are nearly twice as likely to have Internet access as single-parent White households (44.9% versus 23.4%). Black families with two parents are nearly four times as likely to have Internet access as single-parent Black households (20.4% versus 5.6%). And, children of two-parent Hispanic homes are nearly two and a half times as likely to have Internet access as their single-parent counterparts (14.0% versus 6.0%).

These differences are modified somewhat when income is taken into account. Nevertheless, even when comparing households of similar incomes, disparities in Internet access persist. At all income levels, Black, Asian, and Native American households with two parents, are twice as likely to have Internet access as those with one parent. For Hispanics and White households with two parents, on the other hand, clear-cut differences emerge only for incomes above $35,000. For these households, Whites are one and a half times more likely and Hispanics are twice as likely to have Internet access.

The Demographies of Access

Age. Age also plays a role in access to information resources. While seniors have the highest penetration rates for telephones, they trail all other age groups with respect to computer ownership (25.8%) and Internet access (14.6%). Young households (under age 25) exhibit the second lowest penetration rates (32.3% for PCs, 20.5% for Internet access). Households in the middle-age brackets (35–55 years) lead all others in PC penetration (nearly 55.0%) and Internet access (over 34.0%). The contrasts among age groups are particularly striking between rural seniors (23.3% for PCs, 12.4% for Internet) and young, rural households (27.7% for PCs, 13.3% for Internet) on the one hand, and urban 45–54 year-olds on the other (55.3% for PCs, 36.5% for Internet).

Region. The region where a household is located also impacts its access to electronic services. The West is the clear-cut leader for both computer penetration (48.9%) and Internet access (31.3%). At the other end of the spectrum is the South at 38.0% for PC penetration and 23.5% for Internet access. Looking at the degree of urbanization, the lowest rates are in Northeast central cities (30.4% for PCs, 18.7% for Internet access); the highest are in the urban West (49.2% for PCs, 32.0% for Internet access).

State. As with telephones, computer penetration among states is grouped according to tiers due to the ranges of certainty created by the use of 90% confidence intervals. The top tier ranges from Alaska's 62.4% to Wyoming's 46.1%. The middle grouping is bounded by Arizona (44.3%) and Pennsylvania (39.3%). The low tier includes principally southern states, ranging from Oklahoma (37.8%) to Mississippi (25.7%). Regarding Internet access, the ordering of the states—ranging from Alaska (44.1%) to Mississippi (13.6%)—tracks relatively closely the PC rankings, but often with wider confidence intervals at the 90% level.

In sum, disparities with respect to electronic access clearly exist across various demographic and geographic categories. Similar to telephone penetration, electronic access comes hardest for Americans who are low-income, Black or Hispanic or Native American, less educated, single-parent families (but especially single-female householders), young heads-of-households, and who live in the South, rural areas or central cities. Dissimilar to the phone profile, however, senior "have nots" are less connected in terms of electronic access. And Asians/Pacific Islanders have reached a leading status with respect to computers and Internet access that they have not enjoyed in telephone comparisons.

The Expanding Digital Divide

The chief concern with respect to household computer and Internet access is the growing digital divide. Groups that were already connected (e.g., higher-income, more educated, White and Asian/Pacific Islander households) are now far more connected, while those with lower rates have increased less quickly. As a result, the gap between the information "haves" and "have nots" is growing over time.

The increasing divides are particularly troublesome with regard to Internet access.

a. Divide by Race/Origin

The digital divide has turned into a "racial ravine" when one looks at access among households of different races and ethnic origins. With regard to computers, the gap between White and Black households grew 39.2% (from a 16.8 percentage point difference to a 23.4 percentage point difference) between 1994 and 1998. For White versus Hispanic households, the gap similarly rose by 42.6% (from a 14.8 point gap to 21.1 point gap).

Minorities are losing ground even faster with regard to Internet access. Between 1997 and 1998, the gap between White and Black households increased by 37.7% (from a 13.5 percentage point difference to a 18.6 percentage point difference), and by 37.6% (from a 12.5 percentage point difference to a 17.2 percentage point difference) between White and Hispanic households.

Even when holding income constant, there is still a yawning divide among different races and origins. At the lowest income levels, the gap has widened considerably for computer ownership. For households earning less than $15,000, the gaps rose substantially: by 73.0% or an additional 4.6 points between White and Black households, and by 44.6% or an additional 2.5 points between White and Hispanic households. For the households earning between $15,000 and $34,999, the disparities between White and Black households has increased by 61.7% (or 5.0 percentage points), and 46.0% or (4.0 percentage points) between White and Hispanic households.

For the same period, the increases for the $35,000–$74,999 bracket are much smaller for both the White/Black gap (a growth of 6.4%, or 1.0 percentage points) and the White/Hispanic divide (a growth of 15.2%, or 1.5 percentage points). The most striking finding, however, concerns the highest income level of $75,000 or more. For that income range, the gap between White and Black households has declined substantially (by 76.2%, or 6.4 percentage points), while the gap between White and Hispanic households has grown by 4.9 percentage points.

Education and Income

b. Divide Based on Education Level

Households at higher education levels are now also much more likely to own computers and access the Internet than those at the lowest education levels. In the last year alone, the gap in computer use has grown 7.8% (from a 56.4 to a 60.8 percentage point difference). The divide with respect to Internet access has widened 25.0% (from a 36.6 to a 45.8 percentage point difference). Not all groups, however, are lagging further behind the front-runners. Those with some college education, and those with a high school diploma, are now closing in on those with a college education.

c. Divide Based on Income

The digital divide has widened substantially when comparing households of different incomes. In the last year, the divide between the highest and lowest income groups grew 29.0% (from a 42.0 to a 52.2 percentage point difference) for Internet access. The same trends are recurring with respect to all income levels lower than $50,000. Interestingly, however, the gap appears to be narrowing for the mid-range and upper income groups. Households earning between $50,000–$74,999 are now actually closer (by 0.4 percentage points) to those at the highest income level than they were in 1997.

Middle-income households are faring far better with regard to computers. A significant drop of 11.1% (from a 15.3 to a 13.6 percentage point difference) occurred between the highest ($75,000+) and second highest ($50,000–$74,999) income brackets. And the gaps are also narrowing—though less significantly—for those earning more than $25,000.

The Divide Is Likely to Continue

The Census data reveal a number of trends. On the positive side, it is apparent that all Americans are becoming increasingly connected—whether by telephone, computer, or the Internet—over time. On the other hand, it is also apparent that certain groups are growing far more rapidly, particularly with respect to Internet connectivity. This pattern means that the "haves" have only become more information-rich in 1998, while the "have nots" are lagging even further behind.

As the Internet becomes a more mature and pervasive technology, the digital divide among households of different races, incomes, and education levels may narrow. This pattern is already occurring with regard to home computers. Race matters less at the highest income level, and the gap is narrowing among households of higher income and education levels.

Even so, it is reasonable to expect that many people are going to lag behind in absolute numbers for a long time. Education and income appear to be among the leading elements driving the digital divide today. Because these factors vary along racial and ethnic lines, minorities will continue to face a greater digital divide as we move into the [twenty-first] century. This reality merits a thoughtful response by policymakers consistent with the needs of Americans in the Information Age.

> *"If Americans really want a personal computer and access to the Internet, they can obtain them at very low cost."*

The Information Revolution Has Not Created a Digital Divide

Adam D. Thierer

The digital divide—the gap between those who have access to information technologies and those who do not—does not exist, Adam D. Thierer claims in the following viewpoint. He maintains that government proposals to make personal computers (PCs) and Internet access more affordable are unnecessary because PCs have become as inexpensive as televisions and free Internet access is readily available. In addition, Thierer contends that efforts by telecommunication companies and major private-sector employers have helped ensure that all Americans can participate in the information revolution. Thierer is the director of telecommunication studies at the Cato Institute, a libertarian think tank.

As you read, consider the following questions:
1. How much did the cost of a new personal computer system fall between 1996 and 1999?
2. According to Helen Chaney, Internet access has spread how much more quickly than access to television?
3. Why does Thierer believe consumers should not be given vouchers for computer systems?

As the public-policy debate over America's so-called "digital divide" intensifies, federal, state and local policymakers are considering steps to solve an apparent gap between the technological "haves" and "have-nots." Using heated and even some apocalyptic rhetoric, many policymakers in the Clinton administration and in Congress are calling for the creation of new federal entitlements to address what some perceive as a national civil-rights crisis. As Eric Cohen, managing editor of the *Public Interest*, noted in the *Weekly Standard*, "The digital divide is now the hottest social-policy issue in Washington. It's the 'new new thing' in civil-rights politics." Dozens of national solutions to this supposed crisis have been proposed in recent months.

For example, the Clinton administration has proposed a wide variety of new federal programs and more than $2 billion in new spending initiatives in its fiscal 2001 budget. Vice President Al Gore has floated a package of proposals, while members of Congress debate a variety of proposals ranging from tax credits for the voluntary donation of computers to needy schools of individuals to the creation of new federal programs. One proposal would provide direct tax credits of up to $500 to subsidize the purchase of a new personal-computer, or PC, system by low-income families. Another would create a New Deal–type program resembling the Rural Electrification Administration, providing $3 billion in low-interest loans to companies to deploy high-speed broadband networks to rural or remote sections of the United States.

Before policymakers make any rash decisions on these proposals or create expensive new government programs to address America's supposed digital divide, they would be wise to take a closer look at the current market for personal computers and Internet access. Americans live in an age of technological abundance, with a virtual digital deluge of opportunity. Free computers and free Internet access are helping to fill the digital gap. Clearly, the vibrant PC market is doing more than an adequate job of speeding computing technology to every American.

Still, proponents of new programs and spending initiatives to address America's supposed digital divide have articulated their concerns in divisive and quite extreme terms.

National Association for the Advancement of Colored People (NAACP) President Kweisi Mfume has claimed "technological segregation" exists in America, and the Rev. Jesse Jackson has said the digital divide represents "classic apartheid." Not surprisingly, politically charged claims such as these led President [Bill] Clinton to organize a digital-divide summit earlier [in 2000] where the president called for more than 400 companies and nonprofit organizations to sign a "National Call to Action to Bring Digital Opportunity to Youth, Families, and Communities."

Regrettably, these claims and actions assume that a genuine digital-divide crisis exists today in America that demands a national solution and expensive federal entitlement programs to solve. Before policymakers make such a rash judgment, however, they should consider the following evidence, which illustrates how the so-called digital divide is just high-tech hype and hysteria:

Costs Are Decreasing

• *PCs are becoming more affordable.* PC prices have fallen rapidly during the last 15 years. According to computer-research firms PC Data Inc. and Forrester Research, the average price of a new PC system has fallen from $1,747 in 1996 to $916 in 1999 and will fall to an estimated $577 by 2002. More importantly, much less expensive "entry-level" or "budget PCs" are available from major retailers, catalog companies and online vendors for less than $400 and, in some cases, free with mail-in rebates and other special discounts.

• *PC systems are being given away.* Many companies virtually are giving away PCs in exchange for nominal monthly fees and/or long-term service agreements. Today, these systems, which typically include a monitor, keyboard, speakers, a modem and Internet access, only cost consumers between $21 and $29 a month—less than your monthly cable bill.

• *Some PCs are cheaper to buy than TVs.* Prices in the PC market have fallen so rapidly, in fact, that it is not uncommon to find new computer systems that are cheaper than new television sets. This begs an obvious question: If Americans can purchase an Internet-ready PC for less than the cost of a new TV set, just how real is the digital divide? After all, according to the U.S. Department of Energy, 98.7 percent of all Americans—including 97.3 percent of all poor households—own a television set. If virtually every American household can own a TV, which usually will be more expensive than an entry-level PC system, then the need to create an expensive new entitlement program to solve a problem the marketplace is handling so effectively on its own is dubious.

Subsidies Do Harm

Giving Internet subsidies to low-income households would, of course, have several negative consequences. For one, it would cost telephone customers a bundle. The federal government already requires all telecommunications carriers that provide interstate telecommunications services to contribute to a universal service fund to subsidize Internet access for schools and libraries. These carriers receive bills from the universal service administrator based on their interstate and intrastate end-user telecommunications revenues. [In 1998], the price tag for Internet subsidies could reach $2.25 billion for schools and libraries alone. This cost is passed on to telephone customers in the form of higher fees—approximately $6 per customer according to *Internet News*. Extending Internet subsidies to low-income households would make telephone service still more expensive.

Gary T. Dempsey, *Freeman*, April 1998.

• *Internet access is cheap, and often free.* Free Internet access regularly is offered by advertising-supported Internet service providers, or ISPs, which means consumers who already own a PC can sign up for Internet service for no additional monthly fee. More-sophisticated Web portals are reasonably priced at flat, all-you-can-eat rates of roughly $9.95 to $19.95 per month.

• *Many companies offer free computing services.* Other free computing and Internet services are becoming available as well. For example, free e-mail services are quite ubiquitous on the World Wide Web. Additionally, consumers have access to free storage sites on the Internet to save large amounts of information or files on independent company servers and hard drives. This means consumers do not necessarily need to purchase a hard drive of their own to store their files. Also, consumers can access many free software and technical support sites.

• *Emerging hybrid computing systems may soon make PCs irrelevant.* Thanks to the existence of so many free Internet services, consumers increasingly are using new hybrid systems known as "Internet appliances" or "dumb terminals" that offer them instantaneous Internet access without requiring them to purchase a hard drive. For as little as $99, consumers can purchase a keyboard and monitor with built-in Internet software to directly access the Web. Finally, handheld PC devices are becoming increasingly popular, offering another inexpensive technology that could one day be as ubiquitous as cellular phones.

Access Has Increased

• *Companies are rushing to deploy state-of-the-art broadband networks to the home.* Telecommunications network providers are rushing to provide consumers a variety of technological options for accessing the Internet and online networks in general. For example, high-speed digital subscriber line, or DSL, systems are being rolled out by telephone companies, and cable firms are deploying modems to offer fast Internet access through cable systems. More important, wireless Internet technologies are emerging that offer Internet access without requiring a physical wire running into the home, making Internet access available to many more rural Americans in the very near future.

• *Employers increasingly are offering free or subsidized PCs to employees.* Many large private-sector employers are offering their employees subsidized PCs and free Internet access. For example, Ford Motor Company, Delta Air Lines, American Airlines and Intel Corporation announced plans to offer these services to their combined 604,000 employees. This new workplace benefit is likely to become more prevalent as employers compete for quality workers.

• *Free markets are spreading new technologies more quickly than subsidies.* PCs and Internet services already have spread quite rapidly throughout society without government planning or subsidies. As Helen Chaney of the Pacific Research Institute notes, "Internet access has spread to 50 million people in only four years. That's about nine times faster than radio, four times faster than the personal computer and three times faster than television. At this rate, it won't be long until all of those who desire Internet access will have it." By contrast, subsidized technologies such as electricity and basic phone service took much longer to spread throughout society.

The facts presented above illustrate that policymakers need not fear that some Americans may be left behind in this profoundly dynamic Information Age. If Americans really want a personal computer and access to the Internet, they can obtain them at very low cost. Moreover, this trend toward lower-cost PCs and more access is only likely to increase. Expensive federal entitlement programs will not facilitate this process; in fact, they might actually make things worse by putting pressure on computer prices to hold steady or increase.

What the Government Should Do

Proposals to offer consumers $500 vouchers for computer systems are particularly unwise when consumers can obtain them for hundreds of dollars less. It would be tantamount to giving every American a $20,000 subsidy for a new automobile when models are available for less than half that price. Furthermore, if indications are right that the world is entering a post-PC era in which various types of technologies will be used to communicate and access the Internet without requiring a hard drive, then current efforts to subsidize the diffusion of personal computers will limit many people to technology that quickly becomes outdated.

To the extent any government involvement is needed, it is to remove any tax and regulatory roadblocks that discourage companies in the free market from offering consumers the new products and services they demand. More importantly, government officials need to address the real divide problem in this country first—the educational divide. Children, and even many adults, lack the basic educational skills necessary to compete in a digital world and use digital technologies competently. Just throwing a computer in front of a child or an illiterate adult isn't going to magically solve any of our societal problems.

The peddlers of all the digital-divide, high-tech hype should be ashamed of themselves for shifting the nation's attention away from important issues such as these and toward less significant matters such as access to computer technologies and the Internet. But if that's all they're concerned about then they can rest easy because each and every American today has access to an amazing array of digital opportunities. As a *Computer Shopper* magazine article on the rise of the free-PC market fittingly concluded: "[I]t's becoming increasingly clear that the free-PC movement has come a long way in a relatively short time, and it obviously benefits consumers who wouldn't otherwise be able to afford a Net-connected computer. And that's a very good thing indeed."

> *"I think the Internet will be to the 21st Century what the automobile was to the 20th."*

The Internet Has Transformed the Economy

Robert J. Eaton

The twentieth century was dominated by the so-called "Old Economy," which emphasized manufacturing and industrialism. The twenty-first century, however, is being dominated by the "New Economy," which depends on computers and other modern technologies. In the following viewpoint, Robert J. Eaton, former chairman of DaimlerChrysler Corporation, contends that the Internet will be the driving force of the New Economy. According to Eaton, use of the Internet eases communication between companies and enables customers to learn more about products in which they are interested. He asserts that the New Economy will not replace the Old Economy approach to business but will instead make it more efficient.

As you read, consider the following questions:
1. According to the author, what is the effect of business to business e-commerce?
2. Why does Eaton argue in favor of posting negative information about DaimlerChrysler products on the company's website?
3. In the author's view, what are the important economic tools of the Internet?

It's an honor to be [at the Forum Club of Southwest Florida]. The invitation left the topic open, so I decided to talk about the New New Economy. I'm not exactly sure what it is yet. The New Economy, of course, is the Internet economy. The New New Economy is going to be whatever the Internet economy spawns, and that's still the subject of a lot of exciting speculation. . . .

Creativity and Chaos

Now, if you are a cybernetic layman like me, who has spent his entire career in the conventional business world, then Silicon Valley, the Internet, the Digital Age, and the New Economy seem to contradict a lot of what we always thought were fundamental truths.

I went to work right out of college for General Motors (GM). It was the paradigm for the modern corporation. It valued predictability. It abhorred confusion. It rewarded loyalty. It had a very long horizon.

In the New Economy, chaos is considered creative. Horizons are short. There is no deference paid to your elders. The young eat the old. Every successful company in Silicon Valley seems to beget a more successful one that destroys it.

The GM I grew up in did not tolerate mavericks. [Netscape founder] Jim Clark would not have succeeded at GM. I don't know most of you, but I'll venture a guess that the Jim Clarks of the world would have been misfits in most of your organizations.

The Internet Changes Everything

Today, the misfits are those who hang on to those old paradigms. The Internet is the foundation of this New Economy and the key to understanding it. It's impossible to overstate the impact of the Internet. We had a tag line to one of our advertising campaigns a few years ago: This Changes Everything! We were talking about a pickup truck so I guess we were guilty of stretching a little bit to make a point. But when you apply that line to the Internet, there's no stretch at all. It simply does change everything.

It is now, or soon will be, the single most important factor in commerce, in communication, in education, in medicine and every other field that requires human interaction.

Very soon, if you aren't computer literate, you won't be literate. Today, it's a convenience to do your banking on your computer. Soon, it will be a necessity.

It changes everything. The *New York Times* used to be a newspaper. I don't know what to call it now, but it's different. I'd like to have been in the meeting when some lunatic first proposed putting all the paper's content on the web so anybody could get it free. It would be like me giving away cars. Except it made sense.

The New Economy means whole new ways of doing business.

Business to business e-commerce means that from now on corporate structures will be built around the transaction. That used to be the last thing on a planning model. Now it's the first, and everything else will be a slave to the transaction because the company that does the most transactions most efficiently and most accurately rules in the New Economy.

For several years now, our suppliers have been able to do business with us on the Internet. Pretty soon, it will almost be the only way.

The Internet and the Automobile Industry

DaimlerChrysler, Ford, and General Motors got together and created a single Internet trade exchange through which all our suppliers will have to go to reach us. It will create tremendous efficiencies, and eventually become a separate new company. Four or five years ago, our company web site was a toy. We did one because everyone else was doing one, but we didn't understand what it would become and neither did the others. We do now. It will become the primary—and in some cases the only—way to communicate with our customers, our suppliers, our dealers and even our own employees.

Originally, our web site was a combination bulletin board, product brochure, phone directory, and events calendar. But it is rapidly becoming our principal place of business. It's our office. It's our showroom. It's our engineering lab. Notice I didn't say "virtual." We have to start thinking of it as our "real" office.

We have something called "Get a Quote" on our site. It

gives customers all the details about a vehicle they decided they were interested in, and it then sends an e-mail to a nearby dealer to get an actual quote. We found that 45 percent of those customers who got a quote actually bought a car or truck.

We are in the process of putting all the information that a customer may want on the site. Even competitive information. Even negative information about our own products. Why? Because if the customers don't get the information there, they'll get it somewhere else. And once we have them in our site, we don't want them to leave. For any reason! Remember, this is now our place of business!

A Number of Economic Benefits

The evidence [on the Internet's economic effects], when cumulated, leads to the following broad conclusions:

• The *potential* of the Internet to enhance productivity growth over the next few years is real.

• Much of the impact of the Internet may not be felt in e-commerce per se, but in lower costs for quite mundane transactions that involve information flows—ordering, invoicing, filing claims, and making payments—across a wide range of existing "old economy" sectors, including health care and government.

• The Internet produces considerable scope for management efficiencies in product development, supply chain management, and a variety of other aspects of business performance.

• The Internet will enhance competition, both increasing efficiency and reducing profit margins throughout the economy, but the profit squeeze itself should not be counted as a productivity enhancement.

• The Internet is improving consumer convenience, increasing choices, and leading to other benefits that may not be readily measured, or if they are, may show up as productivity gains in industries or sectors other than those in which the savings may be initially generated.

Robert E. Litan and Alice M. Rivlin, eds., *The Economic Payoff from the Internet Revolution*, 2001.

Customers will still go into a dealership and kick a tire or two. The dealer will be just as important as ever as he or she closes the deal and provides the service. Dealers are not going to become extinct. Customers are not going to order a car from us on the Internet and have UPS deliver it. But the Internet will be the principal way they learn about our products, and it will be their principal tool in making a purchase decision.

One of our competitors did something historic [in February 2000]. Ford announced that it was giving every one of its employees—350,000 of them worldwide—laptop computers to take home.

Their reasoning was simple: If you are going to communicate effectively with your employees, then they must all have a computer in the home. As a way of affirming the importance of the Internet to its business, this move sent a strong message.

The Importance of Productivity

By the way, since I see a few car guys here, let me digress just a minute and say something about the auto industry. If the Internet makes your head swim these days, so does Detroit. We think the industry will grow at a slightly faster rate in the future than it has in the past. But we'll move along that trendline with tremendous volatility.

That volatility is basically the result of excess capacity and competition. The market is at an all time high, but so are incentives. We used to put incentives on the products as the market was tanking. No longer. It's part of the cost of doing business. And the customer should be happy about it because the net transaction price increase he or she has paid for a new car or truck over the past three years has been flat—no increase.

That tells you pretty clearly how important productivity is today. And it helps explain the consolidation that has taken place and that will continue. The industry is healthy and more vigorously competitive than ever before, but it's changing. You'll see more and more strategic partnerships as companies try to leverage their own strengths and find new ones. It's changing—fast.

I think the Internet will be to the 21st Century what the automobile was to the 20th—the single most important driving force in the worldwide economy. And the single most important development in terms of changing the way people live and work. . . .

Effects on the Old Economy

What's the real economic bottom line of the New Economy? Is it e-mail? Chat rooms? Family web sites that remind you that Aunt Margaret's birthday is coming up? I don't think so. Those are the toys.

The tools are 3D graphics, and split-second financial analyses, and network data bases, and all the thousands of business to business (B2B) opportunities now being explored.

The real bottom line of the New Economy is going to be its impact on the Old Economy. The Old Economy is going to be the biggest beneficiary of the New Economy.

When I said that the Internet is going to be the automobile of the 21st Century, I don't mean that the automobile is history. It's not. It's going to be here. But the Internet is going to allow us to build it more efficiently. It will be more affordable.

The New Economy isn't going to replace the Old Economy; it's going to make the Old Economy better.

"The claims that [the Internet] is creating a new economy based on information and communication are pure hype."

The Internet Has Not Transformed the Economy

Dwight R. Lee

In the following viewpoint, Dwight R. Lee maintains that the importance of the Internet in modern economics has been exaggerated. He argues that while the Internet is an important technological advance that has made it easier for people to communicate, the free-market economy has always been based on the spread of information. According to Lee, the prices of goods and services in market economies are determined by communication between suppliers and consumers. For example, when consumers are dissatisfied with a product they buy less of it, sending a clear message to the company that made it that the product must be improved. Lee contends that although the Internet is responsible for marginal improvements in the market economy, market prices play a more important role. Lee is the Ramsey Professor of Economics and Private Enterprise Economics in the Terry College of Business at the University of Georgia in Athens.

As you read, consider the following questions:
1. According to Lee, what is essential in order for people to participate in voluntary exchange?
2. As explained by Lee, what prompts consumers to buy products?
3. What do incentives provided by market prices help ensure, in the author's opinion?

Dwight R. Lee, "Internet Is Not Making a New Economy," www.cato.org, July 6, 2001. Copyright © 2001 by Cato Institute. Reproduced by permission.

The Internet is clearly a marvelous technological advance, allowing hundreds of millions of people from all over the globe to exchange information almost instantly. But the claims that it is creating a new economy based on information and communication are pure hype. Long before the Internet we were benefiting from an amazing network of global communication and information in the old free-market economy. There is nothing new about an "information economy."

Why Market Economies Work

Market economies have always been information economies. The Internet can improve the information transmitted through markets, but that information has always been the reason for the amazing success of free-market economies. Let's admire the Internet for the marginal improvements it makes to our market economy. But while admiring the shine let's not ignore the shoe.

Every day each of us simultaneously exchanges messages with millions upon millions of people through the market network. The information we transmit is picked up quickly by those who can best use it, informs them on the appropriate action to take, and provides them the means and motivation to take that action.

The result is a pattern of global cooperation that finds each of us serving the interests of millions of others by using our time and talents to provide what they value most, while benefiting from their reciprocal consideration. This market network has been enriching the lives of those people lucky enough to live in free economies long before the advent of the Internet.

Communication in the market network takes place through prices based on private property and voluntary exchange. Private property is essential for people to engage in voluntary exchange, and when exchange is voluntary it typically takes place at a price that reflects the highest value of what is being exchanged (people generally sell to those willing to pay the most).

So market prices communicate the value others place on the things we own, and motivate us to relinquish those things to others when they are worth more to them than to

45

us. Similarly, market prices for goods and services also reflect the costs of making them available. People will not consistently sell a product at a price less than the value sacrificed to make it available.

Unimpressive Productivity

Just three broad sectors—finance, real estate, and insurance; wholesale and retail trade; and business services—account for about 80% of all computers used in industry. According to the New Economy productivity spin, the not-actually-so-impressive productivity rate will accelerate as information technology spreads to the rest of the economy. But as economist Robert Gordon has shown, productivity growth has been lagging in precisely the industries that form the information-technology vanguard.

Phineas Baxandall, *Dollars & Sense*, May/June 2002.

So market prices communicate how much value is given up elsewhere in the economy to provide products, and motivates us to buy products only when the additional unit is worth more to us than the sacrifice our purchases impose on others.

Firms are constantly listening to the market messages of consumers that are sent in the form of profits and losses. Consumers inform firms with profits when those firms are using resources to produce more value than those resources are producing in other activities, and they respond by expanding their production. On the other hand, consumers inform other firms with losses that they are not providing enough value to cover their cost, and those firms respond by producing less.

I'm not arguing that market prices are the best form of communication for all occasions. How do you say "I Love You" with a market price? Very clumsily. But market prices are far and away the most persuasive way to communicate your desire for chocolates and roses, which will increase the impact of—and payoff from—saying "I Love You."

Improved Communication

Of course, the Internet has made it easier to order those chocolates and roses, but it's the incentives provided by market prices that insure the cooperation of the literally thousands of people who have to coordinate their efforts to get them to you when and where you need them.

Let's give the Internet credit. It is making important changes in our lives and the way we do business. Certainly the Internet is improving market communication in important ways. But without the market network we would all be impoverished by our inability to communicate and cooperate with the millions of people we depend on every day, no matter how much access we had to the Internet.

"Electronic telecommunication . . . increases our overall capacity for social interaction."

The Internet Promotes Social Interaction

William J. Mitchell

In the following viewpoint, William J. Mitchell argues that the Internet encourages a variety of social relationships. He asserts that as individuals become more interested and bonded with each other using electronic media, they inevitably desire more face-to-face meetings. Moreover, according to Mitchell, the locations of Internet connections in coffeehouses and libraries can further social interactions. Mitchell, a professor of architecture and media arts and sciences and the dean of the School of Architecture and Planning at the Massachusetts Institute of Technology in Cambridge, is the author of *E-Topia: "Urban Life, Jim—But Not As We Know It,"* the source of the following viewpoint.

As you read, consider the following questions:

1. What are some of the advantages of online meeting places, in Mitchell's opinion?
2. In the author's view, when are "virtual communities" most successful?
3. What are some of the advantages of Internet cafes?

Experience has shown . . . that putting your thoughts online is not the same as putting your body on the line in places like the Roman forum, Hyde Park Corner, Tiananmen Square, or the Venice Beach Boardwalk. This has both advantages and dangers.

The Freedom of Online Life

Most obviously, online meeting places insulate you from physical risk. You cannot be beaten up by those who take violent exception to your views. There are no muggers, and no cops with billy clubs. You will not be confronted face to face by aggressive panhandlers, or by the mentally ill. This sometimes creates the ground for positive interactions that would not occur otherwise; in Santa Monica, California, for example, the Public Electronic Network (PEN) civic network—which is accessible both from private homes and offices and from kiosks in public places—has provided a congenial, nonthreatening place for the homeless population and their more fortunate fellow citizens to open up a dialogue. Instead of cruising the personals in the *New York Review of Books* or the *Boston Phoenix*, adventurous lonely hearts can take their chances with jailbabes.com—a pen pal and singles introduction service for women "confined in prisons and correctional institutions all over the country." Even more dramatically, citizens of mutually hostile nations, who have no place to meet in physical space, can often find neutral ground in cyberspace.

Furthermore, you are not compelled to display the usual markers of age, gender, and race. You can hide behind your handle or avatar, and you can readily construct disguises and play roles. So, many online hangouts are like masked balls or Mardi Gras celebrations; they provide well-bounded, socially useful opportunities to experiment with self-representation and alternative identities, and to step temporarily into the shoes of others.

But these liberating affordances can also be put to less desirable uses. Anonymity, and the lowered likelihood of retribution, can encourage ranting and flaming. Loudmouths can blather on endlessly from cyber-soapboxes. And disguises can cloak con men and predators.

So it is far too simplistic to think of online meeting places as direct substitutes for physical ones. Instead, we should treat them as useful new additions to the architect's and urban designer's repertoires—with strengths and weaknesses that fit them to certain purposes but not to others.

Widening Social Circles

Whatever their norms and forms—and these will probably remain highly varied—online meeting places will allow circles of *indirect* social relationships to widen. Most of these indirect relationships will be tertiary in character—with corporations and bureaucracies rather than particular persons you can name. (When you purchase a volume from an online bookstore, for example, you do not get to know anyone personally, but you do become economically linked to the anonymous employees of that enterprise.)

In other words, you will be able to keep in some sort of contact with many more people, and these people will be spread over wider areas. According to [computer analyst] Michael Dertouzos's arithmetic, you could quickly reach maybe a couple of hundred people, back in the days of the village, by walking. The automobile jumped that by a factor of a thousand. Now, computer networks push it up a thousandfold once more—to somewhere around two hundred million. You can quibble about the exact numbers, but the orders of magnitude are surely correct.

In this context, you cannot rely—as inhabitants of small towns and neighborhoods traditionally have—upon repeated face-to-face contact to establish the trust on which intellectual and commercial life depends. Nor do you have the benefit of familiar architectural cues; the dignified stone facade of the local branch bank, for example, with its comforting intimations of solidity, permanence, and reliability, is replaced by the interface of an online home banking or financial management system. So, as Internet marketeers quickly figured out, trusted brand names and brokers play an increasingly crucial role. For organizations with goods and services to offer, maintaining brand equity on the information superhighway serves essentially the same purpose—in a much larger context—as maintaining conspicuous premises on Main Street.

Digital telecommunication thus extends and intensifies the earlier effects of transportation networks, mail systems, the telegraph, and the telephone. It serves as a mechanism for economic and social integration on a large geographic scale, cutting across traditional political borders. It proliferates tertiary social relationships, and the associated mechanisms of branding and broking. And Manuel Castells [in his book *The Rise of the Network Society*] has suggested that it may also be "a powerful medium to reinforce the social cohesion of the cosmopolitan elite, providing material support to the meaning of a global culture, from the chic of email addresses to the rapid circulation of fashionable messages."

All this would have astonished grumpy old [Henry David] Thoreau, who—rooted in a nineteenth-century conception of local community—wrote in 1854: "We are in great haste to construct a magnetic telegraph from Maine to Texas; but Maine and Texas, it may be, have nothing to communicate." We know now that they do, indeed, have plenty.

Invisible Boundaries

Paradoxically, though, this globalizing effect is accompanied by the creation of new, less visible boundaries. To see why, let us put Dertouzos's figures in perspective. If you live to a good age, you have maybe half a million waking hours. If your world of interaction is at a village scale, each member of it gets, on average, a couple of thousand hours of your time. At an automobile scale, it is down to two hours each. And at a global computer network scale, it is reduced to less than ten seconds. Clearly, then, attention becomes a scarce resource, and intervening attention management mechanisms are essential if we are not to be overwhelmed by the sheer scale at which electronically mediated global society is beginning to operate.

Mailing lists, newsgroups, personalized news services, information filters of various kinds, software agents, and other arrangements for sustaining and managing online relationships play this crucial role. Reasonably enough, they typically provide efficient means for linking up like-minded people rather than for confronting differences. Advertisers, political activists, and others with messages to get out welcome them, of course, because they effectively segment audiences and markets. Thus they tend to reinforce sociocultural boundaries and categorical identities—as professionals in specialist scholarly areas, members of religious sects, sharers of sexual identities, promoters of political causes, sufferers from specific diseases, cocker spaniel owners, Linux hackers, frequent fliers, Buick dealers, cigar smokers, Trekkies, Barbie doll collectors, or whatever.

It is far too facile, then, simply to equate communication with community (despite the fact that the terms have the same Latin root) and to conceive of cyberspace as some sort of vast village green in the sky. The effects of online interaction are various, complicated, and sometimes socially and culturally contradictory. While they are breaking down some established categories and boundaries, online meeting places can simultaneously strengthen others, and even create new ones. And they are clearly creating a condition under which individuals position themselves less as members of discrete, well-bounded civic formations and more as intersection points of multiple, spatially diffuse, categorical communities.

Increased Face-to-Face Interaction

Of course, time spent interacting online is time spent not doing something else. It is easy to leap from observing this to the conclusion that surfing cyberspace substitutes for more socially desirable face-to-face interaction with family, neighbors, friends, and urban strangers in public places—a chestnut that has routinely been tossed out by recovering netheads, OD'd screen-starers, and computer-jaded curmudgeons. They picture us all huddled at home in our underwear, typing email messages to one another. Under this neo-Durkheimian[1] scenario, anomie rules as never before.

But this reasoning depends on the questionable assumption that our capacities for social interaction are fixed, and thus set up zero-sum games for us; if you devote your attention to certain social opportunities, you must correspondingly decrease your attention to others. There is growing evidence, however, that electronic telecommunication both

1. Émile Durkheim was a French social theorist.

increases our overall capacity for social interaction and changes the structure of the game in complex ways. The consequences are far from straightforward.

Computers Can Foster Human Contact

William Gibson, whose 1984 novel, *Neuromancer*, pioneered the notion of virtual living, now says that electronic communication provides a "sensory expansion for the species by allowing people to experience an extraordinary array of things while staying geographically in the same spot." Gibson warns, however, that the virtual can only augment our physical reality, never replace it. He applauds the countermovement toward what has been called skin—shorthand for contact with other humans.

People who correspond with each other electronically often feel the need for skin and try to meet in what they call real life. Karen Meisner, while an undergraduate at Connecticut's Wesleyan University, was playing a computer game on the Internet in early 1991. During the game she met Pär Winzell, a student at Sweden's Linköping Institute of Technology. He knew her by her game name, Velvet. They began to exchange electronic messages outside the game, sharing thoughts with more directness and intensity than would have been possible in the early stages of a "real-life" relationship. Karen knew something special was happening; they discussed meeting each other. It seemed scary. Then Karen sent an e-mail: "I'm coming to meet you." They have been married for two years.

Technology can also foster skin contact between those who live near one another. Senior citizens in Blacksburg, Virginia, use their computers not only to chat but also to organize get-togethers. "It's like wandering into the town center to meet friends and to check the bulletin board," says Dennis Gentry, a retired Army officer. "Only you can do it in pajamas anytime you want."

Joel L. Swerdlow, *National Geographic*, October 1995.

It seems, for example, that so-called "virtual communities" work best when they are allied with the possibility of occasional face-to-face encounters, and that online interaction actually stimulates demand for more familiar sorts of meetings and meeting places. In his lively account of the early online community the Well, Howard Rheingold observed: "The

WELL felt like an authentic community to me from the start because it was grounded in my everyday physical world. WELLites who don't live within driving distance of the San Francisco Bay area are constrained in their ability to participate in the local networks of face-to-face acquaintances. By now I've attended real-life WELL marriages, WELL births, and even a WELL funeral." And Stacy Horn, founder of New York's Echo, has similarly suggested: "If someone you talk to online is at all interesting, you want to meet them. It isn't so much what they look like, you simply want to be with them *in the flesh*. I don't just want to talk about movies with people, I want to go to movies with people."

In a broader context, the growth in telecommunications during the 1980s and 1990s has—seemingly paradoxically—been accompanied by burgeoning demand for hotel meeting facilities and convention centers. Some of this, no doubt, has simply been due to general economic expansion. But much of it results from a characteristic behavior of geographically distributed businesses, professional organizations, and interest groups; they form and sustain themselves by means of electronic telecommunication, then they find that they need annual face-to-face get-togethers to refresh relationships among members and to reestablish trust and confidence. And conversely, face-to-face contacts at these meetings stimulate subsequent telecommunication. The two are inextricably intertwined.

Comparison of telecommunication and transportation demand statistics tells a similar tale. Generally, the two track in parallel. Unsurprisingly, if you make a lot of long-distance calls, you are also likely to fly to quite a few face-to-face meetings. You can get a lot of bandwidth, when you really need it, by transporting heads attached to shoulders.

Locations of Connection

These interactions of virtual and physical meeting places unfold differently when electronic connectivity is scarce and when it is abundant. And the locations of connection points matter.

When MIT created its pioneering Athena computer network, for example, workstations were few and expensive, and for security and ease of maintenance they were grouped at locations called "Athena Clusters." These soon became important centers of socialization among students, not because they were specially attractive places to hang out (far from it!), and not because students had nowhere else to go, but because they were points of availability of a scarce resource. They functioned much like the village wells of old. Then, when connectivity became far more widely available, their social role began correspondingly to fade.

Similarly, Internet cafes, which provided workstations and refreshments in a convivial setting, experienced a brief burst of popularity when the Internet and the World Wide Web were growing rapidly in popularity but home and office connections were still unusual. They had the additional advantage that working at the computer (like reading a newspaper in more traditional cafes) provided an ostensible reason for spending time in a public place, while observing the passing scene and finding opportunities to meet people. As connectivity became more commonplace, these establishments typically sought to retain their clientele by providing faster connections and machines, unusual and costly types of devices that few would own themselves, and specialized knowledge. And they continued to provide a service to computer-savvy young budget travelers, who used them as an inexpensive means to remain in email contact.

In developing countries (and in poorer areas of developed ones), where the development of high-speed telecommunications infrastructure is likely to lag and where few can afford their own connections and equipment, such public points of access are likely to retain their magnetism for a much longer time. In particular, networks of small, Internet-linked local libraries—along the lines of the Brazilian city of Curitiba's famed Lighthouses of Knowledge—seem particularly promising devices not only for delivering a valuable service, but also for promoting positive social interaction.

Where opportunities for connectivity are abundant, the locations of these opportunities may still be socially significant. If a university simply wires dormitory rooms, for example, it will almost certainly encourage students to stay in their rooms working at their computers, reduce general social interaction, and raise the incidence of conflicts among roommates. But if it goes for laptops rather than desktop devices, provides lots of connection points and power outlets in social spaces and library reading rooms, and implements a dynamic network addressing scheme that allows plug-and-play work anywhere, it will promote mobility among different hangouts, chance encounters, and informal grouping.

"It is not hard to find antisocial sentiments among some of the Net's most dedicated users."

The Internet Discourages Social Interaction

Andrew L. Shapiro

In the following viewpoint, Andrew L. Shapiro claims that the rising popularity of the Internet has been accompanied by the fraying of communal relationships. He maintains that use of the Internet can cause individuals to disengage from public life and give users a narrow view of the world. Shapiro contends that users often forget the importance of face-to-face contact with the people in their community and often report feeling more isolated and depressed as Internet use increases. Shapiro also asserts that relationships formed online tend to be weak and can be severed too easily. Shapiro is a journalist, lawyer, and the author of *The Control Revolution: How the Internet Is Putting Individuals in Charge and Changing the World We Know*, the source of the following viewpoint.

As you read, consider the following questions:
1. Upon what does civilization depend, in the author's opinion?
2. According to Shapiro, how might the Internet threaten the integrity of communities and nations?
3. What feelings are exacerbated by Internet use, according to the HomeNet study?

Andrew L. Shapiro, *The Control Revolution: How the Internet Is Putting Individuals in Charge and Changing the World We Know*. New York: PublicAffairs, 1999.
Copyright © 1999 by Andrew L. Shapiro. Reproduced by permission.

The control revolution . . . is about who shapes our daily experience—the information we are exposed to, the people with whom we interact. Once individuals had little control over this type of experience. In preindustrial societies, it was dictated largely by agrarian work and traditional communal living. Information generally circulated orally and human interaction was bounded by geography and rigid custom. The advent of the printing press meant a gradual transition beyond experience based solely on observation and the spoken word. By reading, one could "experience" events far away—and do so with far greater selectivity, choosing to read one text instead of another. But few individuals could read and most were subject to the whims of monarchs or nobles.

With the end of feudalism and the beginnings of mercantilism, populations became more mobile and people were able to interact with a wider cohort of individuals. This expanded the range of individual control over experience. Eventually, with the birth of industrialism came the rise of urban centers and mass media such as newspapers and magazines. These developments, along with universal public education, provided individuals with the ongoing common experience that helped foster the nation-state and nationalism—a broader sense of community based in part on shared information and interaction. In many developed nations, radio and television played a central role in defining a national culture, pulling together disparate geographic regions and individuals separated by class, ethnicity, language, and race. These mass media helped to create what cultural anthropologist Benedict Anderson calls "imagined communities," simulacra of what humans had when they lived a more clannish existence.

Civilization Depends on Communication

The point of this thumbnail history is simply that community has always been shaped by common information. As the biblical story of the Tower of Babel warned, civilization depends on shared experience, a collective vocabulary of referents that members can draw upon as they interact and try to remain committed to mutual goals. This is obvious if we think about the building blocks of a culture: language, custom, ritual, myth, religion, law, art, and so on. All rely on facts, ideas, and narratives that describe the shared history and destiny of a band of individuals, that help to answer the question, Who are we? Without shared information, two people cannot come close to answering that question the same way.

In less abstract terms, we are all familiar with the way in which shared experience creates affinity, even if the experience is seemingly trivial. Upon meeting someone new, we are inclined to ask questions that might establish a common link. *Where are you from? Where did you go to school?* And when we speak with members of our own communities, what we talk about is often local—having to do with politics, sports, the economy. Without realizing it, we rely in these conversations on shared information that comes largely from common media sources. *Did you see that article in the paper today? Hear that game on the radio?* Back when communities were smaller and less transient, people relied on direct sensory experience for this community talk. *Have you seen Johnson's farm? It's been untended for weeks!* But as our communities grew in size, this dialogue necessarily began to rely on the shared experience provided by mass media.

As the mass media have replaced the common market, town square, and local saloon or café as primary sources of information, the owners of newspapers and broadcast outlets have gained a huge amount of power over social discourse. Certainly, there has been ample reason to criticize publishers and broadcasters for being excessively commercial and inattentive to the public interest. Yet for all their shortcomings, the mass media also united communities. A generation or two ago, powerful news organs like the *New York Times* and CBS—[former executive director of the Christian Coalition] Ralph Reed's "liberal gatekeepers"—may have fed us a homogenous view of the world, but at least they gave us a common frame of reference as we stood at the proverbial water cooler discussing the day's issues. These mass media provided "a kind of social glue, a common cultural reference point in our polyglot, increasingly multicultural society," according to media critic David Shaw. We could assume that our fellow conversants would be exposed to at least some of the same information. We might even assume some sense of common destiny.

The Pitfalls of Personalization

The personalization ethic[1] presents a direct challenge here, as it is intrinsically opposed to common information. [MIT professor] Nicholas Negroponte's example of a customized newspaper that largely ignores a Libyan invasion of the U.S. may be exaggerated. Yet it is telling because it gives us a glimpse of how diverse our information environments are becoming and how this variety may create distance between individuals living within the same geographic communities.

As we know from television today, the more time we spend online, the less time we will have to interact directly with our families, our neighbors, and other community members. But there's a new wrinkle: whereas once the time we spent watching television—or reading a newspaper or magazine—might have provided some sort of shared communal experience (although a poor substitute for face-to-face interaction), personalization provides just the opposite. We may share good times with others online who enjoy the same narrow passions as we do. But the bonds between ourselves and our fellow citizens might become frayed, possibly to the point of breaking.

If members of the Christian Coalition, for example, shunned mainstream news and entertainment, as Reed suggested they should, they might wind up with a pretty skewed view of the world. But, even more, it would be increasingly difficult for Christian Coalition members and nonmembers to get along. The same is true, of course, whether we're talking about the Christian Coalition, the Libertarian Party, or the National Association for the Advancement of Colored People (NAACP). A lack of shared information would deprive different groups of a starting point for common dialogue.

Without even considering the advent of the Net, many social observers already have warned that communal relationships have weakened in recent decades due to hyper-

1. An individual's ability to control the information he or she receives from the Internet.

individualism, changing patterns of work and social life, and the decline of local associations such as labor unions, religious groups, Parent-Teacher Associations (PTAs), and fraternal associations. As a result, Americans appear to spend less time with their neighbors and trust one another less. [Sociologist] Robert Putnam lent these (much debated) observations an indelible image in the title of an influential essay on the subject, "Bowling Alone." Individual disengagement from public life, he warned, is diminishing social capital—that intangible asset that holds communities together, making our lives secure and meaningful. The excessive customization of news, entertainment, and social interaction would only deplete it further.

Ammer. © 1997 by Wiener Zeitung. Reprinted by permission of Cartoonist & Writers Syndicate.

Like the threat to individual well-being, this potential for oversteer stems from our ability to exercise a new degree of control over personal experience. In pre-cyber days, as a disciple of one group or another, I may have become ensconced in a world of parochial information and interactions. But it would have been essentially impossible for me to control with perfect precision all the stimuli I received. I would have had to go to great lengths, for example, to avoid a large headline on a newspaper's front page or a breaking news announcement on television. It would, in fact, have been so difficult that I might not even have tried to avoid such exposure. Yet as mediated experience displaces physical contact, total filtering can give us an unprecedented degree of dominion over experience. This means not just getting the news of your choice, but filtering out extraneous facts—as well as interactions with neighbors who are different from you. As historian Theodore Roszak warns, we may retreat into "solipsistic enclaves where the like-minded exchange E-mail with one another and where we choose our own news of a no-longer shared world."

The Dangers to Communities

It is not hard to find antisocial sentiments among some of the Net's most dedicated users. As one put it: "You can create your own universe, and you can do whatever you want within that. You don't have to deal with people." Not dealing with people is, of course, at the heart of the problem. Yet the threat to our communities has little to do with misanthropes and hermits. There will, in any culture, inevitably be some who shun social interaction and obligation. The real concern is that these traits may rub off on the rest of us without our really realizing it. As we take advantage of alluring opportunities to participate in idiosyncratic online communities and to expose ourselves only to the information we want, we could unintentionally build barriers between ourselves and those who live among us. The uniqueness of face-to-face contact—with friends, neighbors, teachers, coworkers, fellow citizens—may be forgotten, as may the subtle pleasure of serendipitous encounters.

There are real dangers here to the integrity of communities and perhaps even nations. Local activists might have difficulty competing with online communities for the attention of their neighbors. As a country, we could have difficulty resolving complex questions when we are all experiencing such inconsistent views of what is going on—in essence, such different realities. With fewer shared experiences and information sources, citizens may feel less of a connection with, and less of an obligation toward, one another.

Indeed, as national boundaries become increasingly permeable and irrelevant to networked life, individuals might have less incentive even to identify themselves as citizens of a certain country. Their minimal commitment could be to vote for policies that benefit themselves rather than for those policies that protect the common good. Internationally, even as the global nature of the Net promises to let us shrink the world, compromise between different nations and peoples may be more difficult if we indulge our desire to narrow our horizons. "In the worst case scenario," as [columnist] E.J. Dionne puts it, "the global village becomes a global Bosnia. . . ."

Online Relationships Are Too Fluid

The paradox in this potential for social fragmentation (which, again, is not preordained) is that one of the wondrous qualities of the emerging Net is the way it allows users to break down boundaries, erase distances, and build alliances. The control revolution . . . is allowing us to hatch new online communities of individuals located anywhere in the world. These associations have great promise, in terms of their ability to educate and entertain, and to promote learning and even political change. But ultimately they don't have the glue that gives real physical communities their strength.

Put aside for a moment the critiques of online interaction that focus on the deficiencies of the medium: for example, the lack of visual cues—which, after all, might be cured by the emergence of video-based online interaction. Focus instead on the absence of *recourse* online for offensive personal behavior. Sure, there are virtual communities from which you can be "banished" or in which you can be "punished" (beware the virtual flogging). But without any real-world consequences, there is a lack of individual accountability that is inimical to the creation of enduring communal bonds. With online communities, then, we may unintentionally substitute ephemeral ties with others far away for the strong ties of our local environment. (The strength of communities depends on factors that don't have much to do with individual choice or personal control. The happenstance of location, climate, and natural resources, for example, creates dependencies between individuals and groups, and thus creates deep, long-lasting communal bonds. Anthropologists have shown that many cultural practices can be traced to the common ecosystemic needs—in other words, the shared adversity—of people living in close proximity to one another.)

It is, in other words, the fluidity of online relationships that makes them weak. It's not just that members can change identities or harass others with impunity. It's that people can exit effortlessly. As Esther Dyson writes in *Release 2.0*, "people who don't like the rules can leave." This is perhaps the most distinct feature of these groups: The ease and convenience of online interaction means that the cost or hassle involved in switching from one to the next is negligible. For me as an individual, this may be a great feature. I can search for the right clique and pick up and move on the moment someone annoys me or I get bored. But it is this very ability to break ties that makes virtual communities ersatz imitators of the real thing. The constant potential for rearrangement may be productive in the short term, but it means that there is little incentive to keep online associations intact.

The Internet's Effects on the Outside World

Some might think that the weakness of these affiliations would ultimately prevent them from posing any real challenge to physical communities. But to the contrary, the ability to meander endlessly from one online gathering to the next, changing habitats on a whim, is precisely the problem. The fact that we can continue exploring and indulging ourselves is part of what makes the virtual life an attractive alternative to getting involved in one's geographic community.

Few people, we can presume, intend to forge weak bonds online and, in the process, distract themselves from local commitments. But technology always has unintended consequences, and social science research is beginning to show how this may be true for the Internet. Researchers who conducted one of the first longitudinal studies of the Internet's social impact, the HomeNet study, were surprised when their data suggested that Internet use increases feelings of isolation, loneliness, and depression. Contrary to the hypotheses they began with, they observed that regular users communicated less with family members, experienced a decline in their contacts with nearby social acquaintances, and felt more stress. Though a number of scholars have criticized the study's methodology, its results were merely preliminary and the authors were careful to say that more research was necessary. Until more conclusive results are available, what's most important is that we take seriously the hazards outlined in the HomeNet study and attempt to prevent them from becoming worse or taking root in the first place.

Periodical Bibliography

The following articles have been selected to supplement the diverse views presented in this chapter.

Phineas Baxandall	"Is the 'New Economy' More Productive?" *Dollars & Sense*, May/June 2002.
Cynthia Beltz	"Internet Economics," *World & I*, January 1998.
Eric Cohen	"United We Surf," *Weekly Standard*, February 28, 2000.
Stephen S. Cohen, J. Bradford DeLong, and John Zysman	"The Next Industrial Revolution?" *Milken Institute Review*, First Quarter 2000.
William H. Davidow	"Technically, Society Is Changing," *Washington Post National Weekly Edition*, June 14, 1999.
Gary T. Dempsey	"The Myth of an Emerging Information Underclass," *Freeman*, April 1998.
Barry S. Fagin	"Intellectual Freedom and Social Responsibility," *World & I*, March 2000.
Issues and Controversies on File	"Digital Divide," July 26, 2002.
Kathy Koch	"The Digital Divide," *CQ Researcher*, January 28, 2000.
Mark Leibovich, Tim Smart, and Ianthe Jeanne Dugan	"A Booming E-conomy," *Washington Post National Weekly Edition*, June 28, 1999.
Peter Levine	"The Internet and Civil Society," *Philosophy & Public Policy*, Fall 2000.
Steven Levy	"Silicon Valley Reboots," *Newsweek*, March 25, 2002.
Andrew P. Morriss	"The Wild West Meets Cyberspace," *Freeman*, July 1998.
Neil Peirce	"Beyond the Digital Divide," *Liberal Opinion Week*, March 6, 2000.
Lee Sustar	"The Myth of the New Economy," *International Socialist Review*, October/November 2000.

CHAPTER 2

Has the Information Revolution Improved Education?

Chapter Preface

The Information Revolution has had a strong impact on education. For example, few research tools are more beneficial to students than the resources available on the Internet. With a few clicks of a mouse, students have access to material unavailable in their local libraries. Ideally, students use this information to help them write more comprehensive reports and essays. However, not every student is equally ethical, as the epidemic of plagiarizing Internet sources indicates.

Plagiarism is hardly new to academics: Students unable or unwilling to research and write their own assignments have often copied directly from encyclopedias or other works. With the Internet, however, students do not even have to leave their bedroom to find material to pilfer. Sara Burnett, in an article for *Community College Week*, suggests that the Internet has actually altered the values of today's students. She writes, "Students raised in the era of Napster, the controversial Web site where millions download free music, simply believe that if it's on the Internet, it's there for the taking."

Two forms of Internet plagiarism exist. The first is when a student lifts material verbatim from websites and online articles and claims it as his or her own writing. In a survey of ten colleges, conducted during the 2001–2002 school year, 50 percent of the responding students admitted to plagiarism. Of those students, 35 percent had combined written and Internet sources, while 7 percent had used solely Internet material. The second form of plagiarism is the use of so-called Internet "paper mills"—websites that sell research papers and essays on dozens of topics. John N. Hickman, writing for the *New Republic*, reports that these sites sell thousands of papers each year. Although paper mill sites issue the caveat that the papers are to be used only as research tools, it is generally understood that this is hardly the case.

Ironically, the Internet has also made it easier for teachers to spot plagiarized works. If a professor believes that a submitted paper is markedly different in quality and style than what a student has written previously, he or she can visit websites such as Plagiarism.org, which compare character strings in suspected papers with hundreds of Internet papers.

Alternatively, educators can also type suspicious sentences into Google and other search engines and find out if there are any online sources containing identical phrasings.

However, some people doubt whether these actions are sufficient. Hickman asserts: "The only real solution to cyberplagiarism . . . is old-fashioned vigilance. Having spent millions of dollars wiring their students to the Internet, universities may have to invest in smaller classes and a better teacher-to-student ratio. A return to some good old analog, face-to-face teaching may be the only way to keep online plagiarism at the fringes."

The Information Revolution has definitely changed the American education system. However, as the rise in plagiarism suggests, those changes have not all been beneficial. In the following chapter, the contributors debate the ways in which computers and the Internet have affected education.

"Technologies offer teachers and students opportunities that would otherwise be extremely difficult to realize in classroom contexts."

Technology Has Improved Education

Margaret Honey

In the following viewpoint Margaret Honey asserts that computer software, Internet access, and other educational technologies have improved the quality of education. According to Honey, these technologies strengthen language, math, and science skills. She also contends that the Internet gives teachers and students access to important historic and scientific material. Honey concludes that government research and funding can help ensure that educational technology remains effective. Honey is a vice president at the Educational Development Center, a not-for-profit organization that researches and develops educational technology. This viewpoint was originally given as testimony before a Senate subcommittee.

As you read, consider the following questions:
1. According to Honey, which two collections have been digitized and placed on the web?
2. What five factors are required in order for educational technology to be effective, in the author's view?
3. What percentage of educational technology funding is federal, according to the author?

Margaret Honey, testimony before Senate Subcommittee on Appropriations, July 25, 2001.

After more than two decades of research on the benefits of educational technology we now have decisive evidence that technology use can lead to positive effects on student achievement. Specifically,

- In studies of large-scale statewide technology implementations, these efforts have been correlated with increases in students' performance on standardized tests.
- Software supporting the acquisition of early literacy skills—including phonemic awareness, vocabulary development, reading comprehension, and spelling—can support student learning gains.
- Mathematics software—programs like Carnegie Learning's Algebra Tutor, for example, that supports experimentation and problem solving—enables students to embrace key mathematical concepts that are otherwise difficult for many students to grasp.
- Scientific simulations, microcomputer-based laboratories, and scientific visualization tools have all been shown to result in students' increased understanding of core science concepts.

In addition, we know that technologies offer teachers and students opportunities that would otherwise be extremely difficult to realize in classroom contexts. Assessment, information access, collaboration, and expression are four areas where educational technologies demonstrate particular promise—and there is a broad consensus among school reformers regarding the central importance of these issues for improving student achievement.

Assessing Technologies

With respect to assessment, technologies have critical roles to play in helping educators to use data effectively and efficiently to improve instruction. Companies like Wireless Generation are pioneering the development of diagnostic software applications that teachers can use in their everyday work to collect learning data that can lead to direct improvement in instruction. These applications can now reside on handheld computers like Palm Pilots, making it possible for teachers to chart student progress over time, identify where a student is having trouble, and modify instruction to help the student succeed. If our goal is for schools to use data to enable all students to achieve, then these kinds of diagnostic assessment tools are essential in helping teachers to do this work effectively.

During the past decade we have seen a tremendous growth in the range of archival materials that are available on the web. Digital archives have been and continue to be developed by museums, libraries, scientific and other archival institutions. These collections are among the most exciting resources driving educational interest in information and multimedia technologies. Collections as diverse as National Center for Supercomputing's Astronomy Digital Image Library and the holdings of the Louvre Museum have been digitized and provide classroom teachers and their students with access to artifacts and information previously available only to specialized scholars or academic researchers. They give teachers and students opportunities to work with an extraordinary array of authentic materials and up-to-date information that would not find their way into classrooms were it not for the growth and development of technologies. Access to this data literally gives all schools—regardless of their geography or wealth—the potential to have libraries of unparalleled collections and connections to the same materials that our nation's greatest universities have.

Technologies offer many other opportunities to teachers and students. Consider, for example, the issue of collaboration. Teachers are the one professional group in our society that is largely isolated from colleagues during the working day. Phones in classrooms are uncommon at best and shared planning time for teachers is rare in most schools. Much of our work at the Center for Children and Technology has focused on using the communications capabilities of the Internet to develop new models for teacher professional development and collaboration that have the potential for providing teachers with networks of support.

We have worked, for example, with the Library of Congress to develop the American Memory Fellows program. This program brings teams of teachers together in both virtual and face-to-face learning communities to develop, test, and publish creative classroom applications that make use of the Library's digitized collections in American History. Teachers learn how to work with primary-source archives that include photographs, pamphlets, films, and audio recordings from American history and culture. Technology makes access to these materials possible and enables teachers to work together to build lesson plans and curriculum for their classrooms.

Helping Children Use Computers

Computer technology is rapidly transforming society. Although the task may seem daunting, we can take [two] steps to help ensure that children use computers in ways that improve their lives now and in the future.

First, we can ensure that children acquire the necessary skills to navigate the digital world effectively and responsibly. Parents, teachers, and other adults who work with children can teach children to make good choices about the time they spend with computers, to be savvy digital consumers, and to seek out software and online content that educates and inspires, not merely entertains. With our guidance and enthusiasm, children can use the computer to learn about other people and parts of the world, for example, as well as to play video games. If use of higher-quality content increases, industry can be challenged more effectively to meet the demand.

Second, we can ensure that children have opportunities to use computer technology more actively to create, to design, to invent, and to collaborate with children in other classrooms and communities. These are types of activities that empower children to play active roles in the emerging digital world, not merely to navigate through it. With the assistance of highly trained mentors, children can learn to use computers to create finger paintings, or to design and build bird feeders, for example, as well as to surf the Web for the lyrics of hit songs.

Margie K. Shields and Richard E. Behrman, *Future of Children*, Fall/Winter 2000.

Technologies also create new opportunities in which kids can express and communicate their ideas. It is no longer uncommon for schools to encourage reports in multimedia format or for students to build web resources that can be used by others. A team of fifth and sixth graders, for example, created a website called "Online Math Applications" which includes information and exploration of math in connection with music, stock market investments, travel, economic projections and history. They use online calculators, stories, problems, simulations and demonstrations to teach their peers. This site and hundreds more have been created by students participating in an academic contest called ThinkQuest.™

Making Technology Effective

There are thousands of examples of work being done in schools with technology that lead to important gains in student learning. What is most important, however, is that we recognize that technology will not result in measurable gains unless the school context is receptive and well organized for technology use. In more than 20 years of work, we have learned a single lesson over and over again—school context is a critical factor in determining the degree to which educators can creatively and deeply use technology. No matter how well designed the technology, how comprehensive the training program, and how creative individual teachers are, if they work in a context that is not supportive of and receptive to the use of technology for instructional purposes the technology will have little impact on students' learning.

We have learned through our work with numerous school districts around the country, that if technologies are to be used to support real gains in educational outcomes, then five factors must be in place and these factors must work in concert with each other.

1. There must be leadership around technology use that is anchored in solid educational objectives. Simply placing technologies in schools does little good. Effective technology use is always targeted at specific educational objectives; whether for literacy or science learning, focus is the key to success.

2. There must be sustained and intensive professional development that takes place in the service of the core vision, not simply around technology for its own sake, and this development must be a process that needs to be embedded in the culture of schools.

3. There must be adequate technology resources in the school including hardware and technical support to keep things running smoothly.

4. There must be recognition that real change and lasting results take time.

5. And, finally evaluations must be conducted that enable school leaders and teachers to determine whether they are realizing their goals, and how to adjust if necessary.

Several decades of experimentation and research in developing educational software have also taught us some critical lessons. To be effective educational software must accomplish three things. It must:

• Build upon what we know from research about the key areas of knowledge acquisition, including both concepts and procedures, which children must master. Carnegie Learning's Algebra Tutor and Wireless Generation's Diagnostic Reading Assessment are both examples of software applications that are substantially grounded in research about how students learn algebra and how they master early literacy strategies.

• Address real challenges that teachers are facing, and make the task at hand easier to accomplish. The most effective software is always developed in collaboration with teachers and is based on extensive research done in classrooms, to ensure both usefulness and effectiveness. IBM's Reinventing Education Partnerships are a very promising model in this regard.

• Be applicable across multiple contexts and multiple curricula by addressing core learning challenges, not curriculum specific skills and tasks. It should not matter, for example, whether my district uses a balanced literacy curriculum or one that emphasizes teaching phonics. Effective educational software should support the processes associated with learning how to read and be applicable regardless of any specific instructional approach.

The Role of the Federal Government

The Federal role in educational technology is critical in two respects: leadership and funding. The U.S. Department of Education's Office of Educational Technology has provided critical leadership in helping promote a comprehensive vision for the effective use of technology in our schools. This office has defined and administered programs, convened national and regional conferences to bring together state and local technology leaders, compiled and disseminated a well-researched library of best-practices information, and put forward two national technology plans.

The Federal Government has also been an essential partner in technology funding. Thirty-five percent of all educational technology funding has been federal. This is a remarkable figure when compared to the 6.6 percent that the federal government contributes overall to education funding. And the results have been pronounced. [In 2000] the Department of Education released the findings of the Expert Technology Panel. Of the two exemplary and five promising programs that were identified, the federal government originally funded all seven. The Department's Challenge Grant Program along with the National Science Foundation made these and many other innovations possible. Other federal initiatives are helping introduce technology into schools of education so that our newest teachers will be effectively prepared to make technology a substantial partner in the learning process. And, of course, the E-Rate program has resulted in the wiring of over one million classrooms, the vast majority of which are in high poverty communities.

I hope you will conclude from my testimony that we are getting measurable results from educational technology, that we know what it takes to make new educational technology programs successful, and that the Federal Government must continue to provide the leadership and funding without which this progress would not have occurred.

I would further hope that the leaders in this room have the vision to realize that the progress we have made has prepared us for an entirely new level of leadership and funding—that it may be time to conceive of an education initiative on the scale of the Apollo Program or the Genome Project. Indeed, I would submit that the top rating given to education issues in every public opinion poll suggests that the American people have never been more ready to be captivated by such a vision.

Within this decade it will be possible to develop the technologies and to expand the capacity of the educational system, such that every day of school—from kindergarten through college—will be an intellectual adventure tailored to each student's particular learning needs. It will be possible for our teachers to see clearly how each child is progressing, and it will be possible to activate all of the resources in school, at home, and in our communities to ensure that no child is left behind.

If we do this, then every other great goal we might set for this country surely will follow.

Thank you.

*"Technology will not . . . propel a poor
student to the honor roll."*

Technology Alone Has Not Improved Education

Andrew T. LeFevre

Computers and Internet access are not a cure-all for American school systems, Andrew T. LeFevre claims in the following viewpoint. According to LeFevre, technology is so expensive that many schools struggle to finance it, although private industry has begun to help with the funding. Moreover, he argues that educational technology alone has not been proven to improve student test scores. He acknowledges that computers have helped increase parental involvement in their children's education but maintains that these technologies will not be truly effective until teachers and students better understand how to use them. LeFevre is the director of the Education Task Force at the American Legislative Council, a bipartisan organization of state legislators who support individual liberty and free markets.

As you read, consider the following questions:
1. What percentage of classrooms are wired for the Internet, as stated by LeFevre?
2. Why does the author favor public/private partnerships for providing schools with educational resources?
3. In the author's opinion, what is the lynchpin of the educational system?

Andrew T. LeFevre, "American Education in the Information Age," *Ripon Quarterly*, vol. 34, Spring 1999, pp. 22–23. Copyright © 1999 by *Ripon Quarterly*. Reproduced by permission.

At a news conference, [former] Vice President Al Gore unveiled the findings from a report by the National Center for Education Statistics, showing that nearly 80 percent of the nation's public schools were connected to the Internet at the end of 1997—more than double the number in 1994. These numbers look encouraging for reaching one of President Bill Clinton's main campaign goals: having every school in America wired to the Internet by the year 2000.

Proponents of increasing technology in the classroom argue that allowing teachers to use the most advanced tools available will help them better teach our children. Technology will help raise students' test scores and close the gap that is growing between American students and students from around the world.

Affording Technology

After spending over five billion dollars during the 1997–98 school year to begin placing computer infrastructures in their schools, school boards are now facing more complicated questions about the role of technology in classroom. How will they continue to pay for the continuing upgrades necessary to keep up with technological advances; how to best use that technology to improve student learning; and finally, will computers and the Internet actually improve student learning?

As with many other areas of education, dollars needed to implement a program is the most significant obstacle faced by schools in their decision-making process. The five billion dollars spent in '97–'98 to connect 78 percent of the county's 80,000 public schools to the Internet seems like a large sum of money. But upon considering that only 27 percent of the classrooms were wired, you begin to grasp the staggering dollar figure necessary to allow every student equal access to a computer and the Internet while at school. And while the federal government, along with many of the state governments, is proposing programs to help schools pay for the necessary equipment, the majority of the cost is still paid at the local level by parents and businesses.

Many school districts located in less affluent areas of our country will not be able to afford providing the same level of technology as their richer neighbors, even with federal and state help. What then can they do to help their students have access to the latest technology? As was the case in the past, private industry often provides an answer. In the late '70's and early '80's, schools were feeling the same pressure to use advancing television technology resources in their classrooms. And much like today, money was a problem. Several companies stepped forward and offered high tech audiovisual systems—at no cost—if a school agreed to show a 10 minute news program, geared towards school age kids, followed by two minutes of advertisements. Today, over 50 percent of schools in our country take advantage of such a program and are able to use the audiovisual equipment in any way they deem necessary.

Kirk. © 2001 by Kirk Anderson. Reprinted with permission.

Today, with the growing use of computers and the Internet in the classroom, companies are once again stepping to the forefront in helping schools meet their education needs. Several companies are offering schools up to 15 PCs, a server and high-speed Internet access along with word processing software at no cost. In exchange for this approximately $90,000 worth of equipment, the school agrees to allow the companies advertisement space on web browsers used by students navigating through the Internet.

Many opponents to these programs claim advertisements in the classroom blurs the lines between public education and private life. However, the fundamental appeal to these types of public/private partnerships is that there is a net gain for both parties involved. Companies provide a service and are able to make a profit while schools get much needed resources that they did not have the funds to purchase. And unlike federal programs, with all the strings that are attached to them, schools are able to use the equipment to best meet the educational needs of their students. The bottom line is that these programs provide much needed flexibility to schools in need of financial assistance. Not every school will, or should, take advantage of the services these companies provide. But the choice is theirs to make.

Not Yet a Panacea

There have been many studies done to show how computers in the classroom positively and negatively impact student performance. What the studies have in common is the agreement that computers alone don't make the difference. Computers have to be in the right hands and used in the right ways in order to raise student achievements. In fact, a study by Harold Wenglinsky of the Educational Testing Service found that most of the nation's schools are not using computers in ways that are linked to better student scores.

Therein lies the biggest problem facing schools: how to best utilize this new technology to teach our children. Many teachers began teaching in classrooms before calculators became a staple of the American student. Now we are asking them to become proficient in the use of technology that is light years ahead of the computers that were first introduced in the mid '80's. Just putting a computer in a classroom and wiring it to the Internet does not mean student scores will improve instantaneously. Computers and the Internet are educational tools just like the black board and textbooks. Teachers are the lynchpin that makes the whole educational system work. Technology will not turn a poor teacher into an educational superstar or propel a poor student to the honor roll.

Energetic and imaginative teachers who currently are able to teach their classes in a manner that motivates and excites their students to higher levels of achievement will find computers and the Internet a valuable new tool in their daily task. On the other hand, teachers who struggle to hold the interests of their students may latch on to computers as a way to augment their meager teaching skills. But just as television is no substitute for parental involvement at home, computers and the Internet will not make up for lack of teaching skills at school.

One of the areas that new computer technology is making a difference in student education is by helping to increase parental involvement in their children's education. Either via a school web site or by utilizing computerized voice messaging, parents can find out first hand what their children are learning about on a daily basis—even see when their home work assignments need to be completed. Parental involvement is one thing that the experts can agree on that has a dramatic impact on how well a student does in school.

Until computers are available in the numbers and time necessary to truly change how students are taught, it will be extremely difficult to determine their effect on educating students. And once the technology is available to all students, it will still be up to the teachers, and parents, to make sure it is being used in ways that will help their children learn.

Learning to Think

We would do well to remember that the ultimate goal of our educational system is to teach our children how to think for themselves. Technology can be a wonderful tool, but a high-speed modem will never replace a quick mind.

*"Distance-learning courses can now be
designed that replicate the face-to-face
communications of classroom instruction."*

The Information Revolution
Has Improved Off-Campus
Education

Kathleen B. Davey

In the following viewpoint Kathleen B. Davey claims that
the Internet is helping "distance learning," or education that
occurs away from campus, reach its full potential. According
to Davey, distance learning has taken several forms throughout history. However, she argues, these earlier approaches,
which included the use of videotaped lectures, did not allow
for timely discussions between students and instructors. In
contrast, Davey maintains, Internet tools such as bulletin
boards and chatrooms allow for such communication while
enabling students to learn at their own pace. Davey is the
dean of instructional technology at Florida Gulf Coast University in Fort Myers.

As you read, consider the following questions:
1. What is the oldest form of distance learning, as stated by
   Davey?
2. In Davey's opinion, why were interactive video systems
   problematic?
3. According to the author, what are the three tools that
   personal computers and networked technologies provide
   to faculty and students?

Kathleen B. Davey, "Distance Learning Demystified," *Phi Kappa Phi Journal*, vol.
79, Winter 1999, pp. 44–46. Reproduced by permission.

D istance learning is frequently held up as a beacon for extending the opportunity for larger numbers and more diverse groups of people to participate in higher education, thus furthering the achievement of their personal, professional, and economic-development goals. However, probably as much confusion and concern surrounds the phenomenon of "distance learning" as does excitement and hope.

Key Claims

• Distance learning is a new and universally desirable phenomenon.

  • Distance learning will totally supplant campus-based learning in the future.

  • Distance-learning methods are ineffective for most university-level learning goals.

  • Distance-learning experiences are inferior to campus-based learning experiences.

Let us examine these claims to develop a more realistic understanding of what distance learning is and what it is not and to make better judgments on its shortcomings and its promise.

A commonly accepted definition of distance learning is any formal educational process that occurs with the teacher and the student separated by either time or distance. A restatement of this definition is any time a teacher defines, constructs, and organizes learning experiences directed toward specific learning goals, outcomes, and experiences that can be accomplished with the teacher and the student(s) separated by time and/or distance, then distance learning is occurring.

How Distance Learning Has Developed

Given the definition above, distance learning clearly is not a *new* phenomenon.

Almost anyone who has completed any formal education has at some time engaged in distance learning. The oldest and most common form of distance learning is probably homework. A teacher constructs a learning activity that can be accomplished without the presence of the teacher, and the student completes it independently, or with the assistance of someone other than the teacher. Typical homework, by itself, does not constitute a distance-learning course, but it does constitute distance learning. In most respects, a distance-learning course can be thought of as a set of carefully constructed homework assignments. Cumulative, acceptable completion of the entire set of assignments constitutes a course for which official course credits can be earned.

The correspondence course is one of the oldest forms of this kind of distance learning. Educators develop learning experiences that can be described in printed materials and completed independently by students who return written assignments. The assignments are graded and returned to the student, and a certain number of these completed and graded assignments constitutes a course. Historically, correspondence courses were most often directed toward technical skills rather than the general-education learning goals of a four-year degree.

However, within four-year and graduate-education programs, another common form of distance learning has been occurring almost as long as institutions of higher learning have existed: the independent study course or program. Most graduates of either a liberal-studies program or a program in graduate studies have taken one or more independent-studies courses. The teacher and the student agree on a set of readings, written assignments, and/or field experiences that are customized according to the student's interests and then completed independently. Except for occasional face-to-face discussions between the teacher and the individual student, most of the instructional experience occurs not in a classroom with other students, but with the teacher and the student separated by time and distance.

Broadcast video and home video playback equipment provided yet another means of constructing a distance-learning course and allowed the learning goals that could be addressed through independent learning to be expanded. During the late seventies and throughout the eighties, telecourses became a common distance-learning format. Several major telecourse development projects were funded during that period by the Annenberg Foundation, the Corporation for Public Broadcasting, and some community colleges and universities. The resulting materials, when used along with a textbook, other print materials, homework assignments, and tests, constituted a course. Through the video medium, several lower-level general-education learning goals were able to be addressed quite satisfactorily as distance-learning offerings.

Challenge to Distance Learning

If this is the case, then one might ask why distance learning or independent study was not embraced more widely by colleges and universities as a means of offering degree programs and by students as a mean of participating in higher education. The answer to this question probably can be found by answering two related questions: Are distance learning methods effective for addressing university-level learning goals? Are distance-learning experiences inferior to campus-based learning experiences?

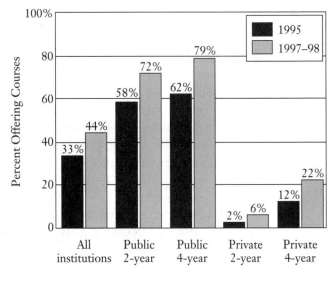

Percent of Institutions Offering Distance Education, in 1995 and in 1997–98

National Center for Education Statistics.

Most university faculty would probably describe the most significant goals of higher education as those that challenge students to examine their held beliefs, to learn to think critically about issues, to generate new solutions to problems, and to develop the written and oral communication skills necessary to contribute to social, political, economic, scientific, and artistic knowledge-building and endeavors. These same faculty would be likely to describe in-class and out-of-class discussions between the instructor and the student and among students as critical to the achievement of these higher-order learning goals. Most university graduates would likely agree that such opportunities for discussion were among some of their most meaningful educational experiences.

Historically and typically, timely discussions between and among students and the instructor have not been possible through correspondence, traditional independent study, or telecourses. Hence, synchronous two-way, interactive video systems (in other words, compressed video systems) excited many faculty during the late 1980s and early 1990s. This technology allows a teacher to be in one location with students at one or more other locations. The sites are interconnected through audio and video networks, and the students at each of the sites see and hear the instructor and vice versa. Correspondingly, several states invested in statewide interactive video communication systems with the promise that salary and capital building expenses could be reduced by using one faculty member to simultaneously teach students at multiple sites throughout a state. Unfortunately, the "interactivity" aspects of these video communication systems frequently turned out to be more video than interactive. The systems also failed to support one of the most desirable attributes of distance learning: asynchronous participation.

The Advantages of New Technologies

The personal computer and associated networked communication technologies have finally provided college and university faculty and students the tools they need to incorporate the convenience and flexibility of time and distance-free learning opportunities with the learning power of effective instructional strategies, such as: 1) student-to-student discussions; 2) faculty-to-student inquiry, clarification, and elaboration; and 3) continuous and timely performance feedback. Thus, almost every two- and four-year college and university in the United States is rapidly developing courses and, in some cases, complete degree programs, that can be delivered and completed using the Internet as the primary communication vehicle.

Using World-Wide-Web-based (www-based) email, bulletin boards, listservs, and chatrooms, distance-learning courses can now be designed that replicate the face-to-face communications of classroom instruction. When these asynchronous, yet interactive, communication tools are combined with web-based information resources, video and audiotaped materials, on-line testing applications, and telephone communications, there are fewer and fewer instructional objectives that cannot be accomplished through distance learning. When carefully planned, constructed, and monitored, Internet-based courses can effectively address many of the same learning goals of campus-based instruction, while allowing students to engage in their learning experiences asynchronously, or according to whatever daily schedule their other personal and work obligations allow.

Will distance learning totally supplant campus-based learning in the future? I think it is probably safe to say not in our lifetime. The learning goals of higher education are diverse and complex, and as such require a diverse and complex array of instructional strategies. Likewise, the learning needs and life circumstances of students are diverse and complex, requiring options for the time, place, and method through which they might participate in higher education. These desired options include face-to-face classes for some purposes and circumstances and distance-learning options for others.

Even so, it is equally safe to say that as we progress through the next century, distance learning will continue to be done:

- more frequently
- through ever-changing methods,
- by a broader range of educational organizations,
- toward a broader range of learning goals, and
- more effectively.

"Attempts to develop cyberspace campuses are doomed to failure."

The Information Revolution Has Not Improved Off-Campus Education

Dave Wilson

Education that occurs outside of schools, often referred to as "distance learning," cannot replace that which takes place in traditional classrooms, Dave Wilson asserts in the following viewpoint. Wilson maintains that students who take online courses are unable to connect with their professors on a personal level and therefore miss out on a vital educational benefit. In addition, he claims that virtual campuses are developed for economic, rather than educational, purposes and do not guarantee to their students a quality education or respected degree. Wilson is a technology reporter and former columnist for the *Los Angeles Times*.

As you read, consider the following questions:
1. How does technology benefit busy students, in Wilson's opinion?
2. According to the author, what distinguishes great educations from adequate ones?
3. Why does Brian P. Copenhaver believe education cannot happen effectively over the Web?

Since the dawn of the Internet age, boosters have predicted the end of leafy college campuses as schools go virtual. The miracle of the Internet was supposed to let great teachers reach any student, any time, anywhere. People all over the world would get the equivalent of a Harvard degree through a computer and a network connection.

What a crock.

"The people peddling this stuff are suggesting that distance learning offers a bona fide education," said David F. Noble, a history professor at York University in Toronto, Ontario, Canada. "But it's a con job. This is a scam. Distance education is just a digital diploma mill."

Not a Replacement

Unlike Noble, I believe that new technologies such as the World Wide Web offer enormous benefits to students. But they work best as an adjunct—not a replacement—to traditional classroom education.

Even tech-heavy institutions such as the Anderson Graduate School of Management at UCLA, where students are required to have a laptop, still consider the classroom the core of the educational experience. Technology helps busy students connect with each other outside of class and gives them access to online resources during lectures.

But attending class solely through a computer isn't a whole lot better than the correspondence courses developed in the 19th century. And even the major universities that offer correspondence courses won't give you a degree. It's the same with computer courses.

"Can you get a University of Chicago degree online? No. Stanford? Columbia? No. They'll offer you certificates, a degree with an asterisk, just like a correspondence course," Noble said. "Because they know the difference."

A Loss of Connection

The difference is obvious to anybody who's had the luxury of learning in a classroom with a couple of dozen people. Compare that with trying to get a professor's attention in a cavernous lecture hall surrounded by hundreds of other students. It only gets worse online.

The ability to connect with a knowledgeable instructor on a personal level is largely what distinguishes a great education from a merely adequate one, or even just a rubber-stamped credential for a better-paying job.

Supporters of virtual colleges point to projects such as the Western Governors University as an example of what the future holds. But WGU is a great example of why attempts to develop cyberspace campuses are doomed to failure.

Quality Is Not Guaranteed

Accreditation has long been the higher education community's alternative to heavy-handed government regulation. It is meant to be a source of quality control and consumer confidence. It is a gateway to federal aid and a conduit for students to transfer academic credits among institutions. And it is intended to augment the value of an academic degree. But few consumers know which accrediting bodies are government sanctioned and which are not. . . .

In such an environment it is simple for ersatz (or merely mediocre) vendors of online course credit to slip by unnoticed. Although several highbrow academic groups have held dozens of solemn conferences on the subject and have published plenty of guidelines, statements of principles, and thoughtful reflections, this corner of American education is essentially unregulated and largely unmonitored. Nobody publishes lists of ersatz electronic degree mills. Nobody rates the good ones and distinguishes them from the snake oil vendors. Caveat emptor.

Chester E. Finn Jr., *American Outlook*, Fall 2002.

The WGU project sprang out of attempts by 18 western states about five years ago to develop a virtual education system to meet the needs of an expanding college-age population. The public selling point for the WGU was better educations for state residents, but the real motivation for a virtual campus is nearly always purely economic. Lawmakers were desperate to avoid raising taxes to pay for the new campuses to accommodate the kids of baby boomers. Many governors listened to the pitch for the inexpensive, more efficient virtual university and eagerly embraced it.

Well, at least at first.

Eventually, most states came to their senses. Aided by budget surpluses and a booming economy, they made at least some extra investments in traditional educational facilities. California was not involved in WGU but instead set up something that evolved into the California Virtual Campus, which largely offers certificate courses received via TV or the Internet. Today, the WGU has utterly failed to achieve its grandiose plans of building a massive university without walls. It remains active on a low level in Utah, offering a way for highly motivated high-schoolers to get a jump on the college-level curriculum. The Internet can indeed let students "attend" a lecture by a professor on the other side of the world. Such lectures are useful and productive. But anybody who suggests that virtual lectures can completely substitute for a classroom experience is selling something—and it's not a first-class education.

An Unsolvable Problem

"I think the face-to-face, person-to-person relationship between student and teacher is irreducible. So it's hard to imagine simply taking the core act of education and making that happen effectively over the Web today," said Brian P. Copenhaver, provost of the college of letters and science at UCLA.

Copenhaver said things might change someday with new technologies. He's a smart guy, but I think he might be overestimating what the technology can do for us. Yeah, at a certain point, it becomes possible for one professor to deliver a lecture over the Internet to a billion students. But how does that one guy answer questions from a billion students? That's a problem better gizmos are never going to solve.

"The E-Rate program is allowing students in
... remote areas to leap into the future."

Government-Sponsored Programs Have Made Computers Accessible to Poorer Schools

William E. Kennard

The E-Rate, or "education rate," program was established in 1996 as part of the Telecommunications Act. The program offers schools and libraries computers and Internet access at reduced rates. In the following viewpoint William E. Kennard lauds the program. He asserts that these lower rates have allowed more than 1 million public classrooms, primarily those in the nation's lowest income areas, to connect to modern telecommunication networks. According to Kennard, the E-Rate program has enabled previously disadvantaged students to prepare for the high-tech economy. Kennard, the former chairman of the Federal Communications Commission, is a managing director at the Carlyle Group, a private equity firm. This viewpoint was originally given as a speech before the Educational Technology Leadership Conference.

As you read, consider the following questions:
1. How many schools and libraries have received funds from the E-Rate program, according to Kennard?
2. In Kennard's view, the E-Rate program combines what two forces?
3. According to a study cited by the author, what percentage of Americans support the E-Rate?

William E. Kennard, "E-Rate: A Success Story," speech before the Educational Technology Leadership Conference, January 14, 2000.

Today the real attention should be on you and your colleagues in the field, the professionals who make the E-Rate happen in our nation's schools.

The E-Rate program began with a vision by President [Bill] Clinton and Vice President [Al] Gore, and Senators [John] Rockefeller, [Bob] Kerrey and [Olympia] Snowe, and Congressman [Edward] Markey. But a vision without application remains just a vision, and it is the people in this room who have moved much of the E-Rate program from vision to reality. When I was in public school, the school technologist was someone who ran the audio-visual machine. They were always popular with the students, because their presence in the classroom usually meant a movie. A movie was something you passively watched, or actively slept through.

A Tremendous Success

Fortunately, times have changed. The movies now shown in classrooms are interactive and computer-based, and your profession no longer takes a back seat in managing education. Now you help drive the whole process, as you have with the E-Rate.

The E-Rate program is a tremendous success, as these amazing figures show:

• Overall, the program has committed $3.65 billion to over 50,000 schools and libraries.

• That means that in the first two years, E-Rate helped connect one million public school classrooms to modern telecommunications networks.

• The program also reduces the "digital divide" between the information haves and have-nots in our society. Fully 70% of the Year Two funding has gone to schools from the lowest income areas, and portions of those funds will reach 70% of the schools under the Bureau of Indian Affairs.

• Finally, the program has connected nearly 13,000 community libraries. Private and Catholic school connections also are impressive: 35,000 and 45,000 classrooms, respectively.

This program is a down-payment on our kids at the beginning of the century that will reap a return on our investment for the rest of this century. It combines two powerful forces—knowledge and the ambitions of our youth—that can continue to fuel the engine of our increasingly high-tech economy.

And comments from the field tell us this:

• In Espanola, New Mexico, the school technology coordinator said the E-Rate has allowed his district "to move into the 21st Century, skipping the whole 20th Century."

• In Fort Thomas, Arizona, a poor, rural area with many Native American students who are learning by computer for the first time, the program's coordinator said, "Our children's future rests on the e-rate. Without it, none of this would be possible."

The E-Rate program is allowing students in these remote areas to leap into the future, and get a crack at the opportunities common to the rest of the nation.

I want to thank the [chief state school officers] for helping make these gains possible. Through your good guidance, we have been able to establish a Year Two funding level of $2.25 billion, and streamline the applications process. That streamlining has included:

• Helping applicants to use state master contracts;

• Accommodating the competitive bidding process to state procurement cycles;

• And customizing forms and improving the on-line filing system.

Some of these ideas have come through the weekly E-Rate teleconference in which you participate, and I hope you will continue to contribute in this way. I realize there is more work to be done on this process, and I welcome your ideas.

Problems Facing the Program

The E-Rate road has not been without its bumps.

Here in Washington, some members of Congress have expressed concern about the pressure the E-Rate puts on everyone's phone bill, relatively small as that amount might be. In 1999 members of Congress introduced six bills to reduce or cut out the E-Rate altogether.

But as an Education and Library Networks Coalition (EdLINC) study found, 87% of Americans support the E-Rate, and 83% of Americans believe that Internet access will improve educational opportunities for our children.

Out in the field, we have to remember that the E-Rate program is not a turn-key program. Connectivity alone does not guarantee educational success.

The Impact of the E-Rate

In 1994 President Bill Clinton called for all public schools to be wired by 2000 and proposed a series of measures to help make that happen. The most important federal initiative has been the Universal E-Rate program, passed under the Telecommunications Act of 1996 and operated through the Federal Communications Commission. This program established subsidies of 20 to 90 percent for school and library access to the Internet—with the largest reserved for low-income schools—funded by a regulatory charge on long-distance telephone service. Spending on this subsidy has totaled more than $2 billion per year. Compared with total computer spending (including hardware, software, training, networking, service) in public schools of $3.3 billion in 1999, the Universal E-Rate program has clearly been very large. It is worth considering its impact on schools.

It is generally not understood by the public how far this program has gone toward wiring schools. . . . In 1994, about one-third of public schools had Internet access and only 3 percent of public school instructional rooms had such access. By 1999, 95 percent of public schools had Internet access and the share of instructional rooms with access had increased more than twenty times, to 63 percent. Moreover, these data show that even among schools where over half the students are eligible for free or subsidized school lunches (that is, low-income locations), more than 90 percent have Internet access.

Austan Goolsbee, *The Economic Payoff from the Internet Revolution*, 2001.

The skills you are called upon to use in introducing new technologies to the schools are demanding, but critically important. Your own conference paper states that if teachers are not trained in using computers, they can hardly be expected to use computers in training their students. Only about one-third of teachers assign computer work to their students on a regular basis.

Teaching effectively through computers cannot be done without connectivity, but E-Rate connectivity is just the first step in a larger process that you in the state departments have to contend with.

Nevertheless, we must keep the success stories in mind.

Your own Hank Marockie, President of the Council of Chief State School Officers, was able to significantly increase students' math and reading skills in West Virginia with the help of computers and integrated learning software. And your conference paper notes that in addition to facilities in West Virginia, advanced broadband networks in North Carolina, Kentucky, Iowa and Texas are contributing to gains in education, workplace training, health and social services.

So it can be done, and the E-Rate program can be your partner in this success. . . .

A Good and Noble Effort

I ask your continued support for the E-Rate, and I hope you will help get out the word on the successes you have generated through that program.

I believe the E-Rate program is one of the most significant programs of modern government, and when the history of the program is written, the contributions of your profession will be in the early paragraphs. . . .

Meanwhile, I can assure you I will work to keep these and other programs that affect education strongly represented at the Commission.

You and I both are in public service. That makes us colleagues in a large and noble cause, although our employer, the public, is not always aware of our efforts.

But I think we can say today that, at least with the E-Rate, the state of our effort is good, and that our employer is pleased.

"There is nothing unique about communications or computing technologies that justifies a federal entitlement program."

Government-Sponsored Programs Are Unnecessary

Adam D. Thierer

In 1996 Congress approved the Telecommunications Act. One element of the act was the E-Rate ("education rate") program, which provides schools and libraries with technology and telecommunications services at reduced prices. Funding for the program comes from taxes on phone bills. In the following viewpoint Adam D. Thierer argues that the federal government should reform what is an unnecessary and costly program. He opines that educational technology should not be funded by hidden taxes and that state and local governments should be responsible for such funding. According to Thierer, unless the George W. Bush administration significantly reforms the E-Rate program, the policy will become an ever-growing national entitlement. Thierer is the director of telecommunications studies at the Cato Institute, a libertarian think tank.

As you read, consider the following questions:

1. Which entity originally administered the E-Rate program, as explained by the author?
2. According to Thierer, what is the annual funding for the E-Rate program?
3. How does Thierer compare the buying of textbooks to the E-Rate program?

You would think that if there were one federal program President [George W.] Bush would want to kill, it would be the "Gore Tax." So named during the presidential election, the "Gore Tax" imposes hidden taxes on phone bills to help wire schools to the Internet. And yet, not only do Bush-administration officials not want to kill this program, they won't even support proposals to limit it.

A Federal Boondoggle

At a March 7, 2001, hearing of the House Education and Workforce Committee, Education Secretary Roderick Paige announced that the administration was backing away from a plan to consolidate the off-budget "E-Rate" program, as it's officially known, into other federal education programs. That's too bad. The E-Rate program is a classic example of an unnecessary and unconstitutional federal program that demands immediate attention before it balloons into a perpetual federal entitlement.

E-Rate is shorthand for "education rate," or the reduced prices for technology and telecommunications services for which schools and libraries are eligible under the program. Championed by former Vice President Al Gore, the program was part of the 1996 Telecommunications Act.

Initially, the E-Rate program was administered by a quasi-government entity, the Schools and Libraries Corporation, formed by the Federal Communications Commission in May 1997 without the consent of Congress. After questions arose regarding the constitutionality of the FCC's creation, the agency shifted responsibility to a non-profit organization known as the Universal Service Administration Company (USAC).

While the FCC's sleight of hand lessened constitutional concerns by seemingly shifting management to a non-profit group, in reality it was business as usual because the USAC takes its orders from the FCC. Consequently, the FCC has continued to demand that the E-Rate program be funded through a complex system of industry mandates and hidden taxes to help lower the costs of installing communications and computer technologies in classrooms and libraries. The FCC has also continued to dictate the amount of annual funding for the program, currently $2.3 billion per year.

President Bush's original proposal to reform E-Rate was modest. The president wanted to make the program marginally more accountable by shifting administration to the Department of Education and requiring a formal appropriation for the E-Rate in the federal budget each year. That got it half right. To the extent that schools and libraries receive public funding for their technology needs, those funds should be incorporated into a formal budget subject to open debate and a vote by elected legislators. Unfortunately, the administration was proposing that these reforms take place at the federal level instead of at the state and local level, where education-spending decisions should occur.

The Poorest Libraries Are Not Helped

When the dust settles, I believe we will find that in many cases the e-rate isn't helping its target audience, the poorest libraries. As Michael Golrick of the Southern Connecticut Library Council wrote on the Universal Services Internet discussion list, "It is axiomatic that the smaller the library (and the greater the financial need) the more important it is for help to be provided."

The 470 [form] alone is six complex pages with 13 pages of fine-print instructions explicable only to people who have some technology training to begin with. Most of the poorest libraries lack the internal or external assistance, the technical acumen, or simply the time to fill out mounds of paperwork on the stray chance some of it will turn into discounts.

Karen G. Schneider, *American Libraries*, March 1999.

The optimal solution would be to end federal involvement altogether and allow the states to operate the E-Rate program on their own, if they so choose. While the jury is still out regarding the sensibility of increased reliance on technology in the classroom, those educational institutions desiring funds for communications and computing services should petition their state or local leaders for such funding, the same way they would for any other educational tool or technology. There is nothing unique about communications or computing technologies that justifies a federal entitlement program while other tools of learning are paid for through state and local budgets.

For example, consider textbooks. Everyone would agree that textbooks are indispensable teaching aids. Policy makers have never suggested, however, the inclusion of a hidden tax in the cost of new novels to help lower the cost of textbooks in the classroom. Such an absurd cross-subsidy would be considered inefficient and unfair. Yet that is how the E-Rate program operates. Hidden taxes on the phone bills of average Americans cross-subsidize school wiring efforts.

It is inexplicable why the Bush administration has decided to surrender on E-Rate reform. Worse yet, the administration's reluctance to pursue serious reform now paves the way for the E-Rate program to become a full-blown national entitlement program. And with time, the burgeoning E-Rate lobby will pressure the FCC to expand the grab bag of high-tech goodies that should be subsidized. Today it's advanced phone service, high-speed Internet access, routers, and hard wiring. Tomorrow, who knows?

There's a perfect candidate to run the E-Rate program in an administration that has abandoned all opposition to it. His name is Al Gore.

Periodical Bibliography

The following articles have been selected to supplement the diverse views presented in this chapter.

Christian Bourge — "No Hyperlinks to Test Success," *Insight on the News*, September 30, 2002.

R.W. Burniske — "Avaricious and Envious—Confessions of a Computer-Literate Educator," *Phi Delta Kappan*, March 2001.

Samuel L. Dunn — "The Webcentric University," *Futurist*, July 2001.

Chester E. Finn Jr. — "Fool U.," *American Outlook*, Fall 2002.

Thomas L. Friedman — "Next, It's E-ducation," *New York Times*, December 17, 1999.

Future of Children — Special Issue: "Children and Computer Technology," Fall/Winter 2000.

John N. Hickman — "Cybercheats," *New Republic*, March 23, 1998.

Issues and Controversies on File — "Distance Learning," March 16, 2001.

John K. Lee — "Ideology and the Web," *Social Education*, April 2002.

Daniel McGinn — "The Internet's Next Big Thing Might Just Be Going to School," *Newsweek*, April 24, 2000.

Bonnie Rothman Morris — "A Day in the Life of the Wired School," *New York Times*, October 5, 2000.

Ed Neal — "Distance Education," *Phi Kappa Phi Journal*, Winter 1999.

Neil Ralston — "Copyright in the Classroom," *The Quill*, July 2001.

Karen G. Schneider — "The Exasperating, Empowering E-Rate," *American Libraries*, March 1999.

Gwen Solomon — "Digital Equity," *Technology & Learning*, April 2002.

Royal Van Horn — "Electronic Scholarship," *Phi Delta Kappan*, November 1999.

CHAPTER 3

Are Rights Threatened in the Information Age?

Chapter Preface

Despite what many people may believe, the content of personal e-mails is not completely private. For example, the FBI is able to access the content of e-mails when deemed necessary to track the movements of suspected terrorists and other criminals. DCS1000, previously known as "Carnivore," is a government device that the bureau uses to retrieve the e-mail of private citizens. If a court grants permission for a wiretap, the device is hooked up to the network of the appropriate Internet service provider (ISP), where it then searches e-mail traffic, looking for names of suspected senders and recipients or certain keywords in the subject line and body of e-mails. Not surprisingly, DCS1000 has raised questions about Americans' right to privacy in the Information Age.

The September 11, 2001, terrorist attacks on the United States have prompted calls for increased monitoring of suspected terrorists' e-mails. Many analysts believe that increased surveillance could enable the FBI to stop terrorist attacks before they occur. Others, however, are concerned that expanded monitoring will result in violations of Americans' right to privacy. University of Southern California professor Bart Kosko, in an opinion piece for the *Los Angeles Times*, writes, "These new laws may well prevent enough terrorism to justify their growing cost. Meanwhile, they have thrust us into a new age of digital surveillance that grows by gigabytes and sometimes terabytes with each linked database. Enjoy your privacy while it evaporates."

In addition to concerns about how Carnivore/DCS1000 might affect privacy, many people question whether the device is even effective. Perhaps the greatest failing of Carnivore took place in March 2000, when an FBI employee destroyed all of the e-mail picked up in a terrorist probe after it was discovered that many of those messages had been written by people who were not being investigated. Unfortunately, those destroyed e-mails included messages written by an alleged member of Osama bin Laden's al-Qaeda terrorist organization—the organization behind the September 11 terrorist attacks.

Americans have always treasured their right to privacy

and other civil liberties. However, as new threats to America's security prompt law enforcement to use increasingly powerful computers to monitor private communications, the sanctity of those rights is being called into question. In the following chapter the authors evaluate the status of personal rights in the Information Age.

"Today's war on privacy is intimately related to the recent dramatic advances in technology."

New Technologies Are a Threat to Privacy

Simson Garfinkel

In the following viewpoint, Simson Garfinkel contends that the Information Revolution has led to a decrease in privacy. According to Garfinkel, websites and other new technologies collect personal data from consumers without ensuring that the information will remain private. Garfinkel asserts that the benefits of technology do not offset this loss of privacy. He concludes that consumers and the government must make concerted efforts, such as establishing a privacy-protection agency, to ensure that one of America's most important freedoms—the right to privacy—is not destroyed. Garfinkel is a columnist for the *Boston Globe* and the author of *Database Nation: The Death of Privacy in the 21st Century*, from which the following viewpoint has been adapted.

As you read, consider the following questions:
1. According to a poll cited by Garfinkel, what percentage of Americans do not research health information online due to privacy concerns?
2. According to Garfinkel, why does privacy-invasive technology not exist in a vacuum?
3. What has been the biggest privacy failure of the American government, in the author's opinion?

A s we move into the computerized world of the twenty-first century, privacy will be one of our most important civil rights. But this right of privacy isn't the right of people to close their doors and pull down their window shades—perhaps because they want to engage in some sort of illicit or illegal activity. It's the right of people to control what details about their lives stay inside their own houses and what leaks to the outside.

Privacy Has Evaporated

Most of us recognize that our privacy is at risk. According to a 1996 nationwide poll conducted by Louis Harris & Associates, 24 percent of Americans have "personally experienced a privacy invasion." In 1995 the same survey found that 80 percent felt that "consumers have lost all control over how personal information about them is circulated and used by companies." Ironically, both the 1995 and 1996 surveys were paid for by Equifax, a company that earns nearly $2 billion each year from collecting and distributing personal information.

Today the Internet is compounding our privacy conundrum—largely because the voluntary approach to privacy protection advocated by the Clinton Administration doesn't work in the rough and tumble world of real business. For example, a study . . . by the California HealthCare Foundation found that nineteen of the top twenty-one health websites have privacy policies, but most sites fail to follow them. Not surprisingly, 17 percent of Americans questioned in a poll said they do not go online for health information because of privacy concerns.

But privacy threats are not limited to the Internet: Data from all walks of life are now being captured, compiled, indexed and stored. For example, New York City has now deployed the Metrocard system, which allows subway and bus riders to pay their fares by simply swiping a magnetic-strip card. But the system also records the serial number of each card and the time and location of every swipe. New York police have used this vast database to crack crimes and disprove alibis. Although law enforcement is a reasonable use of this database, it is also a use that was adopted without any significant public debate. Furthermore, additional controls may be necessary: It is not clear who has access to the database, under what circumstances that access is given and what provisions are being taken to prevent the introduction of false data into it. It would be terrible if the subway's database were used by an employee to stalk an ex-lover or frame an innocent person for a heinous crime.

"New technology has brought extraordinary benefits to society, but it also has placed all of us in an electronic fishbowl in which our habits, tastes and activities are watched and recorded," New York State Attorney General Eliot Spitzer said in late January [2000], in announcing that Chase Manhattan had agreed to stop selling depositor information without clear permission from customers. "Personal information thought to be confidential is routinely shared with others without our consent."

An Unnecessary Trade-Off

Today's war on privacy is intimately related to the recent dramatic advances in technology. Many people today say that in order to enjoy the benefits of modern society, we must necessarily relinquish some degree of privacy. If we want the convenience of paying for a meal by credit card or paying for a toll with an electronic tag mounted on our rearview mirror, then we must accept the routine collection of our purchases and driving habits in a large database over which we have no control. It's a simple bargain, albeit a Faustian[1] one.

This trade-off is both unnecessary and wrong. It reminds me of another crisis our society faced back in the fifties and sixties—the environmental crisis. Then, advocates of big business said that poisoned rivers and lakes were the necessary costs of economic development, jobs and an improved standard of living. Poison was progress: Anybody who argued otherwise simply didn't understand the facts.

Today we know better. Today we know that sustainable economic development depends on preserving the environ-

---

1. Faust was a fictional character who sold his soul to the Devil in exchange for great knowledge. Faust decides to repent toward the end of his life, but the Devil refuses Faust's request and sends the man to Hell.

ment. Indeed, preserving the environment is a prerequisite to the survival of the human race. Without clean air to breathe and clean water to drink, we will all die. Similarly, in order to reap the benefits of technology, it is more important than ever for us to use technology to protect personal freedom.

Most Web Sites Collect Personal Information

The vast majority of Web Sites collect personal information from online consumers, and most collect several types of information, such as name, address, Social Security number and birth date.

Percent of Web Sites Collecting Personal Information

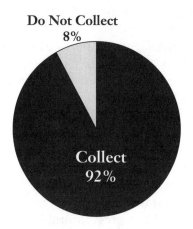

Do Not Collect
8%

Collect
92%

"Privacy Online: A Report to Congress," Federal Trade Commission, June 1998.

Blaming technology for the death of privacy isn't new. In 1890 two Boston lawyers, Samuel Warren and Louis Brandeis, argued in the *Harvard Law Review* that privacy was under attack by "recent inventions and business methods." They contended that the pressures of modern society required the creation of a "right of privacy," which would help protect what they called "the right to be let alone." Warren and Brandeis refused to believe that privacy had to die for technology to flourish. Today, the Warren/Brandeis article is regarded as one of the most influential law review articles ever published.

Privacy-invasive technology does not exist in a vacuum, of course. That's because technology itself exists at a junction between science, the market and society. People create technology to fill specific needs and desires. And technology is regulated, or not, as people and society see fit. Few engineers set out to build systems designed to crush privacy and autonomy, and few businesses or consumers would willingly use or purchase these systems if they understood the consequences.

How Consumers Can Protect Privacy

How can we keep technology and the free market from killing our privacy? One way is by being careful and informed consumers. Some people have begun taking simple measures to protect their privacy, measures like making purchases with cash and refusing to provide their Social Security numbers—or providing fake ones. And a small but growing number of people are speaking out for technology with privacy. In 1990 Lotus and Equifax teamed up to create a CD-ROM product called "Lotus Marketplace: Households," which would have included names, addresses and demographic information on every household in the United States, so small businesses could do the same kind of target marketing that big businesses have been doing since the sixties. The project was canceled when more than 30,000 people wrote to Lotus demanding that their names be taken out of the database.

Similarly, in 1997 the press informed taxpayers that the Social Security Administration was making detailed tax-history information about them available over the Internet. The SSA argued that its security provisions—requiring that taxpayers enter their name, date of birth, state of birth and mother's maiden name—were sufficient to prevent fraud. But tens of thousands of Americans disagreed, several US senators investigated the agency and the service was promptly shut down. When the service was reactivated some months later, the detailed financial information in the SSA's computers could not be downloaded over the Internet.

The Government Must Take Action

But individual actions are not enough. We need to involve government itself in the privacy fight. The biggest privacy failure of the US government has been its failure to carry through with the impressive privacy groundwork that was laid in the Nixon, Ford and Carter administrations. . . .

One important step toward reversing the current direction of government would be to create a permanent federal oversight agency charged with protecting privacy. Such an agency would:

- Watch over the government's tendency to sacrifice people's privacy for other goals and perform governmentwide reviews of new federal programs for privacy violations before they're launched.
- Enforce the government's few existing privacy laws.
- Be a guardian for individual privacy and liberty in the business world, showing businesses how they can protect privacy and profits at the same time.
- Be an ombudsman for the American public and rein in the worst excesses that our society has created.

Evan Hendricks, editor of the Washington-based newsletter *Privacy Times*, estimates that a fifty-person privacy-protection agency could be created with an annual budget of less than $5 million—a tiny drop in the federal budget.

Some privacy activists scoff at the idea of using government to assure our privacy. Governments, they say, are responsible for some of the greatest privacy violations of all time. This is true, but the US government was also one of the greatest polluters of all time. Today the government is the nation's environmental police force, equally scrutinizing the actions of private business and the government itself. . . .

Security and Civil Liberties

Further, we need laws that require improved computer security. In the eighties the United States aggressively deployed cellular-telephone and alphanumeric-pager networks, even though both systems were fundamentally unsecure. Instead of deploying secure systems, manufacturers lobbied for laws that would make it illegal to listen to the broadcasts. The results were predictable: dozens of cases in which radio transmissions were eavesdropped. We are now making similar mistakes in the prosecution of many Internet crimes, going after the perpetrator while refusing to acknowledge the liabilities of businesses that do not even take the most basic security precautions.

We should also bring back the Office of Technology Assessment, set up under a bill passed in 1972. The OTA didn't have the power to make laws or issue regulations, but it could publish reports on topics Congress asked it to study. Among other things, the OTA considered at length the trade-offs between law enforcement and civil liberties, and it also looked closely at issues of worker monitoring. In total, the OTA published 741 reports, 175 of which dealt directly with privacy issues, before it was killed in 1995 by the newly elected Republican-majority Congress.

Nearly forty years ago, Rachel Carson's book *Silent Spring* helped seed the US environmental movement. And to our credit, the silent spring that Carson foretold never came to be. *Silent Spring* was successful because it helped people to understand the insidious damage that pesticides were wreaking on the environment, and it helped our society and our planet to plot a course to a better future.

Today, technology is killing one of our most cherished freedoms. Whether you call this freedom the right to digital self-determination, the right to informational autonomy or simply the right to privacy, the shape of our future will be determined in large part by how we understand, and ultimately how we control or regulate, the threats to this freedom that we face today.

"Many consumers are finding it easier to control their exposure to privacy risks on the Net than off."

New Technologies Are Not a Threat to Privacy

Greg Miller

Despite the claims of the government and media, the Internet is not a threat to Americans' privacy, Greg Miller contends in the following viewpoint. Miller maintains that consumers are more likely to have personal data exploited by non-Internet companies, such as direct marketing corporations, than by websites. He also asserts that websites are more aware than their offline counterparts of the importance of privacy and the need to protect personal data. Miller is a staff writer for the *Los Angeles Times*.

As you read, consider the following questions:
1. By May 1999 what proportion of the most popular commercial sites on the World Wide Web voluntarily posted privacy policies, as reported by the author?
2. According to Miller, why are "cookies" not helpful to traditional marketers?
3. According to Seth Godin, what is more important than possessing data?

Despite the Internet's reputation as privacy's gravest modern threat, consumers are increasingly finding more safeguards on the Net than off.

A study released [in May 1999] offers new evidence of this trend, showing a sharp rise in the number of Web sites that post policies telling people what information is collected from them and how it is used.

Ignoring the Real Menace

Nearly two-thirds of the Net's 7,500 most popular commercial sites voluntarily post privacy policies, according to a statistical sampling of those sites by Georgetown University. That compares with 14% that did so [in 1998] when a similar survey was conducted by the government.

The survey is the latest illustration of how much attention is being paid to the Internet as a privacy menace, an image cultivated in recent years by government summits, congressional hearings and extensive news coverage.

But often lost amid the hand-wringing is the fact that consumers, even tireless Internet surfers, still shed more exploitable data as they wander through everyday life.

Data-driven industries from direct marketing to private investigating remain overwhelmingly dependent on courthouse records, credit card transactions, product warranty cards and other mundane sources. These rivers of offline data keep rising, largely beyond consumers' radar or control.

Impossible as it seems in this digital age, many consumers are finding it easier to control their exposure to privacy risks on the Net than off. And in some ways the Net is spawning enlightened marketing practices that are influencing the offline world. Of course, the Internet is no privacy paradise, and experts agree it deserves ongoing scrutiny. But a growing group of experts are starting to question whether the attention it gets is out of proportion.

The Privacy Rights Clearinghouse in San Diego, for instance, handles hundreds of calls and e-mails every month from victims of privacy breaches ranging from junk mail to identity theft. Almost none of them trace their troubles back to the Net.

"I've often thought of it as a shell game," said Beth Givens, director of the clearinghouse. "Our attention is being diverted to Internet privacy, while there is more impact on individuals from real-world abuses."

Reactions to the Study

That "diversion" continued . . . with the release of a privacy study by the business school at Georgetown University. The report could have wide repercussions at a time when Congress seems increasingly inclined to step up regulation of the Internet.

A bill introduced [in April 1999] by Republican senator Conrad R. Burns would require all commercial Web sites to post privacy policies and to give consumers the opportunity to "opt out" of any collection of their data. [The bill was not brought to a vote.]

Inevitably, groups on both sides of the issue sought to take political advantage of the Georgetown survey, which is loosely modeled on a study conducted [in 1998] by the Federal Trade Commission.

Internet industry groups said the study shows that self-regulation efforts are working and that government intervention isn't necessary.

"We've still got work to do," said Christine Varney, an advisor to the Online Privacy Alliance, which comprises such powerhouses as America Online and IBM. "But this really reflects absolute vindication" for market forces.

Privacy advocates, however, saw evidence that consumers are still far too vulnerable and called for legislative action. They noted that while the study showed a proliferation of privacy policies, few Web sites go beyond that basic step.

Guarding Privacy Online and Offline

Just one in 10 of the surveyed sites adhere to all five elements the Federal Trade Commission (FTC) has identified as essential ingredients of comprehensive privacy policies. By that measure, sites should give consumers notice of what is collected, the choice to opt out, access to collected data, information on security and someone to contact with complaints. "Instead of comprehensive privacy policies, we're getting public relations," said Marc Rotenberg, director of the Electronic Privacy Information Center in Washington.

But beyond this tug-of-war, many consumers wish offline privacy breaches received as much attention.

Roy Segovia, a San Diego computer programmer, barely leaves a trace when he wanders through cyberspace. He guards his identity, wards off marketers' efforts to tag his computer with "cookie" files and avoids online purchases altogether.

But he bought movie tickets over the telephone a few months ago and has been deluged with junk mail triggered by that transaction. "The more I thought about it, the more angry I got," said Segovia, 37. "There are a lot of offline privacy problems we haven't solved yet."

Increased Access to Data

In fact, one of the most overlooked privacy implications of the Net has nothing to do with data collected online but is linked to the market the Net is creating for data that consumers like Segovia give up offline.

"Find Anyone! Only $39.95" proclaims 1-800-USSearch. com, an online Beverly Hills firm that is among the growing ranks of "people finder" services on the Net.

The service does more than just find people. It offers a significant peek into their lives as revealed by the data they shed every day. The firm pulls together property records, auto registrations, magazine subscription lists, telephone listings, corporate affiliations, bankruptcy filings and more.

The company has 150 employees and handles 1,500 searches a day, 80% of them requested through its Web site. The rest are requested by phone.

"This information has been available for decades, but just a select few had access to it," said Nick Matzorkis, the founder of the company. "Companies like ours balance the playing field." Matzorkis said none of the data his company uses are generated on the Net, a claim echoed by direct marketers, private investigators and others.

That is bound to change as millions of consumers continue their steady migration to the online world and as the Net absorbs an increasing share of transactions that have traditionally taken place in person, by phone or through the mail.

But experts say there are widespread misconceptions among consumers about how data collection on the Internet works and that consumers often fret most about information marketers care about least.

Misunderstood Cookies

"There's a perception in people's heads that they are moving about the Net with a homing beacon attached to their backs," said Randolph Court, a technology policy analyst for the Progressive Policy Institute in Washington. "That's just not the way the Internet is." Thousands of Web sites do use "cookies," files that sites place on users' computers to note how many times they visit and keep track of users' passwords and preferences.

The technology is critical to the personalized services that are driving the Internet's popularity. It enables portal sites, such as Yahoo, for instance, to offer personal Web pages that let millions of users see only the weather reports, stock updates and news summaries that interest them most.

But most cookie data are not personally identifiable and consumers can block cookies altogether. Furthermore, traditional marketers say they have no use for this data.

Entrepreneurs Are Sensible

Most large companies do tell you what they will do with information you provide. It should be obvious that the goals of Internet entrepreneurs are pretty simple: To make money, to burnish their firm's reputation, to boost its market valuation. Anything that helps them lure consumers to Web sites and keep them there will help—and entrepreneurs are smart enough to puzzle out if privacy policies and limits on reselling personal information will be attractive or not. In the Internet economy, stock prices are valued with an eye to future visits and future traffic—and there is no single better way to prevent that from happening than losing your customers' confidence by misusing their personal data.

Declan McCullagh, *Liberty*, August 1999.

David Schwartz, president of 21st Century Marketing in New York, compared examining data generated by cookies and so-called "clickstream" analysis techniques to visiting a popular beach. "You'll see a million footprints in the sand," Schwartz said. "If you want to follow one set of footprints, you might see that someone walked down to the ocean and then over to the barbecue area. But it's not something that's relevant."

And besides, there are mountains of offline data to choose from. "Female buyers of pet accessories," and "bow hunters of big game," are among the 28,000 marketing lists available, according to the SRDS Direct Mailing List guidebook.

Much of this data comes from magazine subscriptions, direct mail catalogs and product warranty cards. It is supplemented with more data from real estate records, telephone listings, census surveys and credit histories.

Privacy and Technology

Often the most serious privacy breaches, such as identity theft, happen in low-tech settings, as Saleh Shatnawi discovered when his Social Security number, credit card number and other information was stolen from his health club membership file, which had been left near the club's front counter.

Shatnawi, a restaurant owner in Santa Rosa, California, learned of the breach weeks later when police told him the thief had opened a bank account in his name and was bouncing checks. "It was a real mess," Shatnawi said. "And there was nothing I could do about it." Government officials acknowledge that a disproportionate share of their efforts are aimed at the Internet these days, but say that focus is justified.

"The Net deserves this emphasis," said Robert Pitofsky, chairman of the Federal Trade Commission. "If you ask people why they don't make purchases on the Internet, the No. 1 reason is that they are concerned about privacy."

But the same technology that makes gathering data online so easy also helps activists mobilize consumers against perceived privacy breaches.

Intel and Microsoft, for instance, beat hasty retreats from the consumer backlashes that ensued when their microprocessors and software were perceived as compromising consumers' privacy. And while spam, or unsolicited advertising e-mail, is still a nettlesome problem, it is largely a tool for the disreputable.

"On the Internet, possession of data is not nearly as important as permission to use that data," said Seth Godin, vice president of direct marketing for Yahoo, the Internet's most popular site. "You can buy 60 million e-mail addresses for about $200, but that list will get you in so much trouble, your company will never recover." That kind of hostility to privacy violations is bound to spread offline, Godin said. The Net is not only raising awareness of privacy, he said, but whittling away consumers' tolerance for annoyances from junk mail to dinner time telemarketing.

Perhaps that's wishful thinking, and even Godin acknowledges there is plenty of room for improvement in Internet privacy. But [the Georgetown] survey highlights an interesting disparity.

"Sixty-six percent of all Web sites provide some privacy notice," said Varney. "Do 66% of the entities you deal with offline provide you with a privacy notice?"

"The primary arbiters of what's seen on the Internet ought to be individuals."

Restricting Obscenity on the Internet Threatens Free Speech

Mike Godwin

In 1998 Congress passed the Child Online Protection Act (COPA), a bill that makes it unlawful for material that is "harmful to minors" to be posted on the Internet unless steps are taken to ensure that children cannot access the material. However, in June 2000 the Third Circuit Court of Appeals ruled that COPA is unconstitutional. In the following viewpoint Mike Godwin claims that the Third Circuit was correct to question the validity of COPA because the act's reliance on community standards to determine which material can be considered obscene is problematic for website publishers. According to Godwin, these publishers—whose works reach people throughout the world, not just their own municipalities—cannot guarantee that their sites will meet the standards of the most restrictive communities unless they either severely curtail content or install cumbersome age-identification programs. He concludes that parents should set their own standards and determine which websites their children may visit. In May 2002 the U.S. Supreme Court voted unanimously to temporarily block prosecutors from enforcing COPA. Godwin is a contributing editor for *Reason* magazine.

As you read, consider the following questions:
1. In Godwin's opinion, on what notion is COPA based?
2. According to Godwin, why do social conservatives dislike community standards?

Mike Godwin, "Standards Issue," *Reason*, October 2001. Copyright 2001 by Reason Foundation, 3415 S. Sepulveda Blvd., Suite 400, Los Angeles, CA 90034, www.reason.com. Reproduced by permission.

C hances are that if you're at all acquainted with the arcane legal territory known as "the law of obscenity," you know that in the United States such law is based on "community standards" that shift from one jurisdiction to another: What folks consider obscene—that is, without any redeeming social, cultural, or aesthetic value—in one place may be unobjectionable somewhere else. This is no small matter, as material considered obscene can legally be censored.

Challenging the Child Online Protection Act

What you may not know is that a federal Appeals Court decision has called the entire "community standards" doctrine into question and that the U.S. Supreme Court has agreed to weigh in on the matter. This sets up the possibility of the first wholesale revision of obscenity law in decades. While there are reasons to be optimistic that the outcome will increase the realm of protected speech, there are also reasons to worry that we may end up with fewer speech rights.

Here's the background: In 1998, Congress passed the Child Online Protection Act (COPA), which is aimed at preventing minors from getting access to sexually explicit but otherwise legal material. COPA is based on the notion that the government has a role in preventing children's exposure to content that is legal for adults (that is, material that isn't legally obscene) but that nevertheless might be considered "harmful to minors" (sometimes known as "obscene for minors").

Soon after COPA became law, the American Civil Liberties Union challenged it in court, claiming it overly restricted First Amendment–protected speech. A U.S. District Court in Pennsylvania agreed that COPA ran afoul of the Constitution and, in June 2000, the 3rd Circuit Court of Appeals also agreed that COPA was too restrictive. The Supreme Court has agreed to hear the case in the upcoming term, which begins in October [2001].[1]

Analyzing the Third Circuit Decision

So why is the 3rd Circuit decision troublesome? In *Miller v. California* (1973), the Supreme Court came up with a way of

1. In May 2002, the Court voted to temporarily block the enforcement of COPA.

dealing with so-called obscene content that got the high court out of the business of deciding at a national level what content is legal and what can be punished. *Miller* held that the definition of obscenity depends at least in part on the standards of local communities: Content that is acceptable in New York or San Francisco isn't necessarily going to be legal in Waco or Paducah, the court reasoned. At the same time, the court did carve out an exception for material that has "serious" literary, artistic, or other social value; such content, it ruled, can't be obscene no matter what local standards prevail.

Miller didn't address whether sexual content that's legal for adults is legal for minors as well, but subsequent federal and state court cases have suggested that "community standards" apply here, too. This led to the concept of otherwise legal content that may be "harmful to minors." Thus, parents in Manhattan, New York, may think little of allowing their children access to content that would appall parents in Manhattan, Kansas. As the 3rd Circuit correctly noted in its decision, the statutory scheme of COPA is wrapped around that concept of "harmful to minors," which itself depends on the notion of "community standards."

This, said the 3rd Circuit, is a big constitutional problem for Web site publishers. After all, when you put up a Web site, you can't tell who's going to access it or where they are—at least not with current technology. So even if you publish content on your Web site that isn't harmful to minors in your locale, you can't guarantee that a kid in a more restrictive community won't click his way to it. What COPA effectively requires, the court concluded, is that every Web site operator design his content so that it is acceptable—not "harmful to minors"—in every jurisdiction in the country, or else check everyone's I.D. at the door. Either alternative is excessively burdensome on speakers—especially speakers such as the *Buffy the Vampire Slayer* fans who write erotic fiction featuring their heroine or the keepers of racy Web logs, whose content is not only legal for adults, but also clearly protected by the First Amendment. (COPA purportedly addresses only commercial Web site operators, but the definition of "commercial" in the statute is so broad that it arguably includes even nonprofit and hobbyist Web sites.) Based on this reasoning, the 3rd Circuit concluded that the "community standards" doctrine—at least when applied to the Internet—is itself unconstitutional.

On the face of it, the 3rd Circuit's dismissal of community standards on the Internet should please somebody. After all, the two basic sides in the various legal fights over sexually explicit material both dislike community standards. Civil libertarians find the doctrine too restrictive and variable, while social conservatives hate it because it allows too much to be published (plus, it has that annoying escape clause about "serious" value).

The Future of Community Standards

Despite such problems, the community standards doctrine has brought comparative stability to an aspect of law that had become increasingly contentious. Which is the main reason you can expect the Supreme Court to think long and hard before dumping the doctrine, Internet or no Internet. That, in turn, explains why both sides in the . . . Supreme Court case are wrestling with how to deal with the community standards issue: No one wants to ask the Supreme Court to do what it is plainly loath to do—make national standards and hence deal with every obscenity case in the country. But no one really wants to defend the community standards doctrine, either.

It's likely that the government, along with various social-conservative amici curiae such as the National Coalition for the Protection of Families and Children, will argue for a national "harmful to minors" standard, under which COPA could survive a constitutional challenge. But COPA's defenders may argue something different: that community standards are just fine as a way of regulating content, so now let's make the content providers come up with a technological fix—up to and including redesigning the way the Web works—in order to enforce those standards. COPA's challengers, despite their earlier successes in this case, may want the high court to avoid the community standards issue altogether. After all, they got COPA struck down in the trial court because the law was judged unconstitutionally overbroad and vague in its regulation of speech protected by the First Amendment. Thus, they too may ask the Court to find other reasons to uphold the finding that COPA is unconstitutional. No need, they may argue, to revisit community standards doctrine [in 2001].

No National Consensus

The Child Online Protection Act (COPA) isn't limited to pornographic images online: It encompasses written descriptions of actual or simulated sexual acts that some juries might consider harmful to minors. It's shocking that the federal government is trying to restrict access to text on the Internet—after all, the Supreme Court hasn't allowed the banning of books since the late 1940s. And yet only Justice John Paul Stevens voted to invalidate COPA on these grounds, emphasizing that "because communities differ widely in their attitudes toward sex, particularly when minors are concerned, the Court of Appeals was correct to conclude that . . . applying community standards to the Internet will restrict a substantial amount of protected speech that would not be considered harmful to minors in many communities." But Stevens refused to follow his powerful reasoning to its logical conclusion: Namely, if there is no national consensus about what's obscene for children, there's also no national consensus about what's obscene for adults.

Jeffrey Rosen, *New Republic*, June 3, 2002.

But perhaps there's a way to revisit community standards doctrine and find something useful and pro-liberty in it. It helps to remember that when it comes to censorship, what lawmakers have been trying to preserve is not government authority to regulate content per se, but community integrity—the ability of groups to maintain the character of their public spaces without being confronted with, say, sexually oriented businesses such as adult bookstores and strip clubs.

In other words, lawmakers are interested in public spaces, not private ones. That the government has no authority to invade the privacy of a home to root out obscenity—regardless of community standards—has been established at least since the Supreme Court's 1969 decision in *Stanley v. Georgia*.

With that case in mind, it seems certain that whatever the social interest is in regulating obscene and harmful-to-minors content, it has to do only with public spaces—spaces outside the home. The government's power to regulate obscenity and harmful-to-minors content has been understood in the modern era to be a function of that community interest in protecting public spaces.

So when we look at community standards, what we're looking at is a right that is vested not in state and federal police officers, but rather in the citizens of communities themselves. Historically, that right has been delegated to the police, but the problem in the age of the Internet has been that police-centered content regulation—especially when it comes to content whose legality varies depending on what community you're in and what age the audience is—is too blunt an instrument. And retrofitting the Internet to make things easier for police is too frightening a prospect to accept.

The Internet is a decentralized medium, so it makes sense that the primary arbiters of what's seen on the Internet ought to be individuals, including individual parents. We Internet users tackle this problem in different ways—some of us may use filtering software to enforce our choices, while others, eschewing what they see as the clumsy world of commercial filtering tools, simply rely on their own ability to choose where they go and what they and their children see on the Internet. It's not a perfect system, of course, but it's better than having the cops make their own judgments as to what may be "harmful" to our minors, and it's better than balkanizing the Internet technologically and legally in order to make it easier for the cops.

Is this user-centered approach to community standards a First Amendment framework that we all can live with? In a sense it always has been—it's precisely the system that we parents are used to enforcing in the offline world. All parents know their children will encounter things in the real world that they'd prefer they not see. What we parents have relied on, historically, has been our ability to instill our own community standards in our children—internalized values that remain with our kids when neither parent nor policeman is around.

In that sense, the Internet and the Web don't pose any new community standards problems—just a digital version of a very old one that we've been coping with for a long time.

"This Court has repeatedly held that the government has a compelling interest in protecting children from material that is harmful to them, even if it is not obscene for adults."

Restricting Obscenity on the Internet Does Not Threaten Free Speech

Theodore B. Olson

In 1998 Congress passed the Child Online Protection Act (COPA), which makes it unlawful for material that is "harmful to minors" to be posted on the Internet unless steps are taken to ensure that children cannot access it. In the following viewpoint U.S. solicitor general Theodore B. Olson argues that COPA is constitutional. According to Olson, COPA does not violate the First Amendment because the legislation relies on community standards to determine whether Internet material is harmful. He asserts that because these standards are likely to be fairly constant throughout the United States, the Supreme Court should uphold COPA and reverse the June 2000 ruling by the Third Circuit Court of Appeals, which unanimously ruled that the act was unconstitutional. In May 2002 the Supreme Court voted to temporarily block prosecutors from enforcing the law.

As you read, consider the following questions:
1. In Olson's opinion, how can website operators avoid sending their material to certain geographic areas?
2. According to the author, why is Congress's judgment on community standards unlikely to conflict with the ruling in *Miller v. California*?

Theodore B. Olson, *Supreme Court Debates*, February 2002.

This Court has repeatedly held that the government has a compelling interest in protecting children from material that is harmful to them, even if it is not obscene for adults. The court of appeals in this case [*American Civil Liberties Union v. Reno*] agreed with that fundamental proposition. Furthermore, the court of appeals assumed for purposes of its decision that the Child Online Protection Act (COPA) represents the least restrictive alternative to further that compelling interest, and that there may be no other means by which harmful material on the Web may be constitutionally restricted.

The court nonetheless held that COPA's reliance on community standards to determine whether material is harmful to minors imposes an impermissible burden on protected speech. This Court, however, has long approved the use of community standards as a central component of obscenity and harmful-to-minors statutes, and has viewed them as furnishing an indispensable First Amendment safeguard. . . .

Community Standards Have a Long History

The court of appeals isolated one aspect of COPA's harmful-to-minors standard as constitutionally flawed—its reliance on community standards to help determine whether material is designed to appeal to the prurient interest of minors and is patently offensive with respect to minors. That reliance, however, is not unique to COPA. Community standards have long been a component of obscenity and harmful-to-minors statutes, and this Court has repeatedly approved their use.

The application of community standards in determining obscenity predated this Court's seminal decision in *Roth v. United States* (1957). In *Roth*, the Court upheld the constitutionality of applying "contemporary community standards" to determine whether material is obscene. The statute upheld in *Ginsberg v. New York* (1968) similarly applied to material that was "patently offensive to prevailing standards in the adult community as a whole with respect to what is suitable material for minors." In *Miller v. California* (1973), the Court reaffirmed that, in enforcing obscenity laws, States are free to apply "community standards" rather than a hypothetical "national standard" in determining what is designed to appeal to the "prurient interest" or what is "patently offensive."

And in subsequent cases, the Court has upheld the constitutionality of applying "community standards" in deciding those issues under Federal obscenity laws. State harmful-to-minors laws, including display laws, similarly incorporate "community standards" to determine whether material is designed to appeal to the prurient interest of minors, is patently offensive with respect to minors, or both.

Far from treating community standards as constitutionally suspect, this Court has always viewed community standards as furnishing an indispensable First Amendment safeguard. Early lower court obscenity cases had permitted obscenity to be judged by its effect upon "particularly susceptible persons."—*Roth*. In *Roth*, the Court rejected that standard as inconsistent with the First Amendment, and approved application of community standards as a safeguard against the censoring of works that legitimately address sexual issues.

Businesses Should Conform to Community Standards

The court of appeals acknowledged that community standards could be applied constitutionally in all contexts other than the Internet and the Web. The court held, however, that community standards could not be applied constitutionally to the Web. Based on the determination that there is no technology on the Web that permits a website operator to limit a communication to a particular geographic area, it concluded that applying community standards to the Web effectively means that a commercial website must place behind an age verification screen the material that offends the most puritan community. The court viewed that burden as constitutionally impermissible.

The court of appeals' belief that there is no way for a website operator to avoid disseminating its material to a particular geographic community is incorrect. For example, a Web publisher could obtain name and address information through a registration process, and then mail passwords to the addresses provided at registration, limiting such mailings to the geographic areas of its choice. Even if we accept for present purposes the premise of the court of appeals' holding—that COPA effectively requires Web businesses to conform to community standards throughout the country concerning what material must be placed behind an age verification screen—that consequence does not violate the First Amendment.

Wright. © 1998 by Tribune Media Services, Inc. Reprinted with permission.

There is nothing "unreasonable" about that consequence. When a commercial entity chooses to conduct a nationwide business or to operate on a nationwide medium, like the Web, and to regularly display harmful-to-minors material, it obtains the advantages of a nationwide market for its profit-making activities. It is entirely reasonable to require businesses that have made that choice and that have reaped that economic advantage to make sure that their business activities do not cause harm to minors in the communities from which they seek to profit.

This Court's decisions in *Hamling v. United States* (1974) and *Sable Communications, Inc. v. FCC* (1989) support that conclusion. *Hamling* involved a criminal prosecution for mailing obscene material. The Court upheld the constitutionality of applying community standards rather than uniform national standards to determine the issue of obscenity under that statute. The Court stated that "[t]he fact that distributors of allegedly obscene materials may be subjected to varying community standards in the various Federal judicial districts into which they transmit [their] materials does not render a Federal statute unconstitutional because of the failure of application of uniform national standards of obscenity."

In *Sable*, the Court upheld the constitutionality of the prohibition against obscene telephone messages. The Court rejected Sable's argument that the statute violated the First Amendment because it effectively "compell[ed]" those who operate dial-a-porn businesses "to tailor all their messages to the least tolerant community." The Court read *Hamling* to foreclose the argument that the need to comply with potentially varying community standards renders a Federal statute unconstitutional. The Court further noted that "Sable is free to tailor its messages, on a selective basis, if it so chooses, to the communities it chooses to serve."

The court of appeals sought to distinguish *Hamling* and *Sable* on the ground that the parties involved in those cases "had the ability to control the distribution of controversial material with respect to the geographic communities into which they released it." "By contrast," the court stated, "Web publishers have no such comparable control." As we have pointed out, Web businesses can control—albeit at some expense—the distribution of their materials into particular geographic areas.

COPA's Narrow Focus

The court of appeals' view that community standards cannot be applied constitutionally to the Web was premised in large part on its assumption that COPA's reliance on community standards effectively requires "vast amounts" of worthwhile material to be placed behind adult verification screens. The harmful-to-minors test, however, narrowly cabins the material that is covered by the Act, so that COPA applies primarily to pornographic teasers that appear on the websites of commercial pornographers. Thus, if COPA requires vast amounts of material on the Web to be placed behind screens, it is only because commercial pornographers display so many pornographic teasers.

The serious value prong, in particular, significantly circumscribes the types of material subject to COPA. In *Pope v. Illinois* (1987), the Court held that the serious value prong of the *Miller* obscenity standard does not incorporate community standards. The Court explained that "insofar as the First Amendment is concerned . . . the value of the work [does not] vary from community to community based on the degree of local acceptance it has won." Instead, the proper inquiry is "whether a reasonable person would find . . . value in the material, taken as a whole." Moreover, "the mere fact that only a minority of a population may believe a work has serious value does not mean the 'reasonable person' standard would not be met."

In the context of State harmful-to-minors display laws, that has meant that material is excluded from coverage if it has "serious literary, artistic, political, or scientific value for a legitimate minority of normal, older adolescents."—*ABA*. Thus, pornographic magazines, like *Hustler*, *Penthouse*, and *Playboy*, must be put behind blinder racks, while books that contain serious and informative discussions about sexual acts need not. COPA's serious value prong draws that same line. That component of COPA, entirely ignored by the court of appeals, effectively limits COPA's reach to a narrow band of material.

Other elements of COPA also place legal limits on what may be found to fall within the scope of the statute. For example, material is covered by the first prong—appeal to the prurient interest—only if it is, "in some significant way, erotic."—*Erznoznik v. City of Jacksonville* (1975). That requirement excludes as a matter of law pictures of a nude baby, the nude body of a war victim, or scenes from a culture in which nudity is indigenous.

Similarly, material is covered by the second prong—"patent offensiveness"—only if it falls within one of the specifically defined categories of depictions: "an actual or simulated sexual act or sexual contact, an actual or simulated normal or perverted sexual act, or a lewd exhibition of the genitals or postpubescent female breast." Thus, COPA does not apply to a picture of a scantily clad belly dancer, the typical cover of *Cosmopolitan* or *Vogue*, or scenes from Britney Spears' Pepsi commercial, no matter how erotic some minors might find such depictions.

Community Standards Are Reasonably Constant

The constitutionality of applying community standards to the Web is further supported by Congress's judgment that, on the relevant issues, community standards are likely to be "reasonably constant" throughout the country. The court of appeals cast that judgment aside, finding no evidence that "adults everywhere in America would share the same standards for determining what is harmful for minors."

Congress did not assume, however, that communities everywhere would have precisely the same understanding of what is prurient and patently offensive with respect to minors. Instead, Congress concluded that the standard applied to those issues is likely to be reasonably constant. As applied to the narrow band of material that lacks serious value for a legitimate minority of older minors and is not excluded from coverage under the first two prongs as a matter of law, that judgment is firmly grounded in common sense.

Congress's judgment that community standards are likely to be reasonably constant in the present context does not conflict with the observation in *Miller* that communities throughout the country may vary on whether material is obscene for adults. Even if the average adults in a particular locality or State might feel that adults should have relatively free access to pornographic material, there is no reason to believe that those same adults would want minors in the locality or State to be exposed to such material. Moreover, there is every reason to expect a far greater degree of agreement from community to community concerning what appeals to the prurient interest and is patently offensive with respect to minors on a nationwide and readily accessible medium like the Web.

Congress's direction that juries should be instructed in terms of an "adult" standard rather than a "geographic" standard further promotes a reasonably constant application of community standards. That direction means that juries should not be instructed to consider the community standards of a particular geographic area, such as a city, town, judicial district, or State. Instead, as authorized by *Jenkins v. Georgia* (1974), a jury should be instructed to consider the standards of the adult community as a whole, without geographic specification, concerning what materials appeal to the prurient interest and are patently offensive with respect to minors. . . .

In COPA, Congress responded directly to the Court's concern about the unprecedented breadth and undefined parameters of the Communications Decency Act (CDA). COPA defines harmful-to-minors material in terms that have been well understood since this Court's decision in *Ginsberg*; it does not cover material unless it is designed to appeal to the prurient interest of minors; it specifies the particular sexual acts and parts of the anatomy the depiction of which can be found to be patently offensive; it makes clear that the prurient interest and patently offensive determinations should be made "with respect to minors"; it does not cover material that has serious value for a legitimate minority of older minors; and it applies only to businesses that regularly and for profit display harmful-to-minors material.

| *"Internet piracy is the single biggest*
| *impediment to digital trade today."*

Intellectual Property Rights Require Greater Protection

Bonnie J.K. Richardson

In the following viewpoint Bonnie J.K. Richardson maintains that the U.S. government must work with the entertainment and computer industries to ensure that intellectual property is not threatened by copyright theft. She argues that some trade-based legislation and treaties have helped enforce intellectual property laws. However, Richardson contends that rules formulated by the countries (including the United States) participating in the Hague Convention may not be as beneficial for the copyright industries because American companies might find themselves under the jurisdiction of nations whose laws are contrary to those of the United States. Richardson is the vice-president of trade and federal affairs for the Motion Picture Association of America. This viewpoint was originally given as testimony before the House Commerce Subcommittee on Commerce, Trade, and Consumer Protection.

As you read, consider the following questions:
1. How many movies are downloaded illegally each day, as cited by Richardson?
2. What is "one of the disturbing truths in the e-commerce world," according to Richardson?
3. In the author's view, what are some of the questions of jurisdiction that the Hague Convention fails to address?

Bonnie J.K. Richardson, testimony before the House Commerce Committee Subcommittee on Commerce, Trade, and Consumer Protection, May 22, 2001.

I am testifying on behalf of the Motion Picture Association of America. MPAA is a trade association representing seven of the major producers and distributors of filmed and digital entertainment for exhibition in theaters, for home entertainment and for television. Our members include Buena Vista Pictures Distribution, Inc. (A Walt Disney Company), Metro-Goldwyn-Mayer Studios Inc., Paramount Pictures Corporation, Sony Pictures Entertainment Inc., Twentieth Century Fox Film Corporation, Universal City Studios, Inc., and Warner Bros., a division of AOL Time Warner.

The Jewel in America's Trade Crown

As many of you may already know, the content industries—movies, television programming, home video, music publishing, computer games and software—are America's most successful exporters. These copyright-based industries generate more revenues internationally than any other US industry—more than aircraft, more than agriculture, more than automobiles and auto parts. We also create jobs in the United States at three times the rate of the rest of the economy. As Jack Valenti, President and CEO of the Motion Picture Association of America, is fond of saying, the copyright industries are "the jewel in America's trade crown."

Digital networks offer new opportunities for delivering our entertainment products in international markets. In [2001,] several movie studios will launch new, encrypted online services. No one knows today which business model, or models, will prove most successful in getting digitized entertainment content to customers, but we may start to get some answers in the next few months.

The one thing I can tell you is that all of those business models for the digital delivery of content—at home and abroad—depend on successfully protecting the content against theft.

Preventing Copyright Theft

Internet piracy is the single biggest impediment to digital trade today. Piracy of copyrighted materials is not a new problem. In the last quarter century, MPAA and its associated anti-piracy organizations have spent a billion dollars fighting video piracy and signal theft around the world. At present, we have anti-piracy programs in over 80 countries. What is new in the fight against piracy in the Internet era is the speed and ease with which our products can be stolen and distributed illegally over digital networks. Today, Viant (a Boston-based consulting firm) estimates that some 350,000 movies are being downloaded illegally every day. By the end of [2001], they estimate that as many as one million illegal movie downloads will take place every single day. The scale of the problem is unprecedented.

We have some new tools for combating copyright theft. At the end of 1996 the World Intellectual Property Organization (WIPO) adopted two new treaties to bring copyright standards into the digital age. These treaties clarify exclusive rights in the on-line world and prohibit circumvention of technological protection measures for copyrighted works. The United States Congress implemented those treaties over two years ago in the Digital Millennium Copyright Act. Unfortunately, other countries have not acted quite as swiftly, and the treaties are still not in effect. Twenty-four countries have deposited their instruments of ratification of the WIPO Copyright Treaty; 22 countries have completed the ratification process for the WIPO Performances and Phonograms Treaty. We hope to reach the 30-country mark before the end of the summer so the treaties can enter into effect. [The treaty took effect on March 6, 2002.] Of course, even after the treaties enter into force, we will continue working to get all countries to adhere to these important principles. One of the disturbing truths in the e-commerce world is that piracy flows to the country where the levels of protection are the lowest; even the tiniest country can be the source of extraordinary levels of damage.

Meanwhile, we support the efforts of the Administration to ensure that the standards set in the WIPO treaties and the standards in the Digital Millennium Copyright Act are incorporated into free trade agreements, including those with Singapore, Chile, and the Free Trade Agreement of the Americas.

Swift and vigorous enforcement of copyright laws by countries around the globe is also essential. Tools provided by

Congress for ensuring effective enforcement of intellectual property laws remain extremely important for ensuring that countries abroad provide effective enforcement against piracy. These tools include Special 301 and other trade-related legislation, including the Generalized System of Preference (GSP), the Caribbean Basic Economic Recovery Act, the Caribbean Basin Trade Partnership Act, the Andean Trade Preferences Act, and the African Growth Opportunities Act.

Problems with the Hague Convention

The Hague Convention is also attempting to tackle issues that are very important to any company that engages in international commerce. When laws are broken, which country or countries have jurisdiction over the infractions and where can the judgments be enforced? The Hague Convention is attempting to complete an international instrument to address these questions in a global fashion.[1]

The questions of jurisdiction are especially complex in the e-commerce world. What factors should determine where a transaction or resulting injuries took place? Is it where the company is headquartered? Where the server is located? Where the customer is located? Does it matter whether or not the service is being advertised or directly marketed to customers in a particular country? Does the language in which the service is being offered indicate intent, or lack thereof, to conduct business in a particular country? What does it mean to "target" activities toward a particular forum, and how do U.S. notions of minimum contacts and purposeful availment work in the online environment?

Because copyright theft is such a pervasive international problem—particularly in the Internet environment—and because we rely on courts around the world to help bring pirates to justice, the copyright industries have been particularly concerned about the new rules being formulated by the Hague Convention. A common-sense convention on jurisdiction and the enforcement of foreign judgments could have some benefit to the copyright industries in confronting global infringe-

---

1. As of January 2003, the Convention—in which dozens of nations, including the United States, are participating—had not yet finalized a treaty.

The Problems of Digitization

It has become almost trite to say that digitization presents extremely serious problems for copyright protection. There are, of course, many benefits to copyright owners as well as to the rest of society. Nevertheless, the fact that copyrighted works may be speedily and cheaply duplicated in unlimited quantities and without any degradation of quality even when copies are made from copies, the fact that digitized works may be easily and cheaply transmitted throughout the world by the push of a computer button, and the fact that digitized works may be easily and cheaply modified have created a qualitative rather than merely a quantitative difference in the dangers faced by copyright and, accordingly, in the defenses required for copyright protection. In this regard, it is important to recognize that adequate defense of copyright is needed not only to protect the works themselves and the interests of copyright owners but also to protect those interested in creating and operating the physical infrastructure which depends on copyrighted works for its prosperity.

Bernard R. Sorkin, testimony before the U.S. Copyright Office, May 4, 2000.

---

ments, and we support the United States' efforts to reach such a common-sense solution. Unfortunately, the operative draft of the Convention is painted with a broad brush that reflects the fact that much of the discussion leading up to its creation occurred before the advent of e-commerce. As a result, and by failing to squarely address the types of difficult questions I just raised, the Draft Convention in its current form threatens to do more harm than good.

Some who oppose the treaty have focused on copyright as an example of why the Draft Convention is problematic. They point to differences in national law and the possibility that a judgment rendered in a foreign country based on foreign law will be enforced in the United States. They suggest that the solution is simply to excise intellectual property issues from this agreement. We do not view this as a good solution. The fact is that today—even in the absence of a global convention on jurisdiction—U.S. companies who engage in e-commerce must deal with differences in national laws and can be called into court in a foreign country to answer for acts that reach foreign countries. (The Yahoo! case on the sale of Nazi memorabilia in France is just one example).[2] On top of that, the U.S. is quite liberal in its recognition and enforcement of foreign judgments. This is happening today.

It is important to keep in mind that the Hague Convention doesn't try to resolve questions of substantive law. If substantive laws were the main question, copyright issues would be easier to address internationally than many other e-commerce related problems, such as illegal content or privacy. There is a greater degree of harmonization of copyright laws as a result of the Berne Convention and the WTO Trade-Related Aspects of Intellectual Property Rights (TRIPS) agreement[3] than is the case in many other areas of law and policy. The problem is jurisdiction: Will the Convention result in U.S. companies finding themselves subject to jurisdiction in a forum where they would not be subject to jurisdiction today, and would the Convention result in the enforcement of judgments that today would not be enforced?

These issues of jurisdiction underlie all kinds of tort actions and are of as much concern to other e-businesses as to the copyright industries. The problems cannot be resolved simply by excising intellectual property. The same questions remain with respect to cases for defamation, for hate speech, for privacy violations, for unfair trade practices, and for all other areas of non-harmonized law. We agree with others that the current Draft Convention inadequately addresses these questions, and we believe these questions must be answered with respect to all areas of the law if the Convention is to go forward. . . .

Government Support Is Needed

I want to thank the members of this committee for your keen interest in the barriers that affect digital commerce. The American film, home entertainment and TV programming industry is the only industry in America today that enjoys a positive balance of trade with every country around

2. In May 2000, a French court ruled that Yahoo! must prevent residents of France from accessing sites that sell Nazi memorabilia.   3. The Berne Convention protects literary and artistic works, while the TRIPS agreement requires members of the World Trade Organization to enforce intellectual property rights.

the globe. Together with our colleagues in the music, books and software industries, we are America's leading exporter. With your continued vigilance and support, as you work with the Administration and with foreign governments, you can ensure that America's "crown jewels" continue to sparkle brightly in the digital age.

> *"Over the last ten years there has been an increase in intellectual property protection both on and off the Internet."*

Intellectual Property Rights Do Not Require Greater Protection

James Boyle

In the following viewpoint James Boyle maintains that intellectual property rights, especially those laws that cover material published on the Internet, have become too extensive. He contends that these laws make the Internet overly centralized and regulated and do not encourage the creation of new works. Boyle also asserts that although the Internet does make it easier to copy intellectual works such as music, it also makes it easier, through the use of search engines, for owners of intellectual works to track down illegal copying, thus actually conferring to intellectual property owners a net gain. Boyle is the William Neal Reynolds Professor of Law at Duke Law School in Durham, North Carolina, and the author of *Shamans, Software and Spleens: Law and Construction of the Information Society.* This viewpoint was originally given as a speech before the National Federalist Society, an organization that supports the primacy of individual rights.

As you read, consider the following questions:
1. According to Boyle, how has trademark law changed in recent years?
2. Why does the author criticize the Sonny Bono Term Extension Act?
3. In Boyle's opinion, why should Federalists oppose further expansion of intellectual property rights?

Over the last ten years there has been an increase in intellectual property protection both on and off the Internet. Intellectual property rights have gotten longer, deeper, and wider. Longer in the sense they cover things for more time, deeper in the sense that they cover elements of use that were never previously thought to be covered, and wider in the sense that they cover areas which particular intellectual property regimes—copyright, patent, trademark, and so forth—were never thought to cover. There are some obvious examples—the Sonny Bono Term Extension Act, which increased the copyright term from life plus 50 to life plus 70, the Compilations of Data Anti-Piracy Bill . . . and certain provisions of the Digital Millennium Copyright Act, particularly its anti-circumvention provisions.

Those are merely the most obvious examples—attempts to extend copyright dramatically, or to create entirely new intellectual property regimes of dubious constitutional validity—but there are also other less obvious areas in which intellectual property has expanded.

The Expansion of Patent Laws

Patent law has dramatically expanded both on the Internet and off. The Patent and Trademark Office has taken an attitude towards registration which one might best describe as supine; it would be hard, even for me, to overstate its willingness to give patent protection to "inventions" which seem blindingly obvious, not terribly novel and of dubious utility as well. Priceline.com's sort of business method patents are a wonderful example. Here we have an absolutely fascinating claim; basically patenting the idea of an auction with a reserve price.

There are other expansions in patent law which have received less attention than the business method patents, but which ultimately may become more important. For a long time it was thought that you couldn't patent algorithms, formulae or ideas. Increasingly, for a variety of reasons—some of them legal, some of these technical—those restrictions are being eaten away and, deprived of its restraining conceptual walls, patent rights have begun to expand enormously. One of the most important developments in terms of the Internet is the fact that the Patent and Trademark Office and the courts seem to believe that any program running on a computer—whether it's a program that makes a business method work, or a program that follows through the steps of an algorithm,—becomes a patentable machine. But since almost any algorithm, business method or what have you, can be given a software incarnation, where are the limitations on patentability? . . .

Beyond patent, we have some dramatic expansions of what trademark was normally thought to cover: from a system that encourages investment in brand names that act as reliable and efficient signals to the public, trademark law has morphed into a series of new forms of intellectual property, which have no connection to consumer confusion and which are highly regulative of speech—the anti-dilution provisions, for example.[1]

Understanding the Arguments

I could go on (and on) with such examples, but the basic point is a simple one. There has been a dramatic increase in intellectual property protection over the last ten years. What should you think about all of this? I will argue you today that you should be profoundly unhappy, if you have attachment to any of the traditional Federalist commitments; What are those commitments? Well, as I see them, they are a deep concern with constitutional fidelity, focusing particularly on original intent and original understanding; a skepticism about the Congress's ability to find new forms of Federal legislative power in broad understandings of the clauses of the Constitution; a similar skepticism about the justification and the need for government intervention in the economy and in personal life; and an attempt to measure the costs and benefits of regulation in some kind of relatively rigorous way. My argument would be that each of these ought to lead us to be extraordinarily skeptical about all of the expansions of intellectual property that I have described, particularly on the Internet.

1. Anti-dilution are provisions that determine whether a person who is violating trademark laws must cease and desist his or her activities.

Now what is the other side of the argument? Well, I think the other side of the argument is to say "These are just property rights. . . . We have always been in favor of property rights. This is a property rights issue—it's got nothing to do with speech, nothing to do with regulation, nothing to do with getting the state to prop up established industries from their competitors. What we have here are property rights, which are the basis of the market and that is what we need to protect." That is certainly a valid point of view, but I would say that if you look at what has been happening here, particularly in terms of the expansions that I am describing, that argument simply doesn't cut it. Let's start with constitutional analysis. Congress, as you know, is given power under the Copyright Clause only to create and expand intellectual property in order to promote "the Progress of Science and the Useful Arts." That is to say there is an explicit functional limitation. We can't simply hand over property rights to authors and inventors for fun, or because we like them, or because we think they have invested a lot of effort, or because we want their price-to-earnings ratio to increase. We only can under the Constitution hand over intellectual property rights to authors and inventors when it is necessary to encourage them to produce some new piece of innovative work. The clause also says that Congress can only grant exclusive rights "for limited times"—which, in my view, does not justify Congress's present practice of always trying to keep the Copyright term fifteen years ahead of the Disney copyrights. If we approach eternal copyright terms asymptotically, apparently, the Constitution is not supposed to be violated. I have trouble with that argument.

Also, notice that as the Supreme Court has understood the Copyright Clause, there is a requirement that it only cover original works, or requires some degree of creativity—something that has been held both in the patent and in the copyright realms. This should make us extremely skeptical of new intellectual property rights, such as the Collections of Information Anti-Piracy Act, the so-called "Database Bill," which would create new forms of intellectual property protection over facts and compilations of facts. How do the new intellectual property regimes measure up if we take the Copyright Clause seriously? The best example here is the Sonny Bono Term Extension Act. It is just hard for me to understand how giving dead authors a twenty-year increase in their term can possibly be understood as an attempt to encourage them to produce more works. This strikes me as an attempt by private groups through rent-seeking behavior to get the Government to grant them a monopoly in order to solidify their dominant position in a marketplace and to exempt them from the free market pressures which would otherwise face them. This is a bad thing. It is also constitutionally dubious in my view.

The Economics of Intellectual Property

Federalists have also been much influenced by the economic analysis of law, demanding evidence of the economic justification of any state intervention in the economy, particularly where such interventions amount to the creation of state-protected limited monopolies. Think of airline deregulation. What happens when we apply this kind of skepticism to the expansions of intellectual property, particularly those that are aimed at the Internet? Well the conventional response is that the Internet is a grave threat to intellectual property rights because of the risk of piracy, and hence, the expansions of intellectual property are justified. Let's be clear, the Internet definitely poses a risk of piracy. People can copy programs, "rip" CD's, distribute unauthorized copies of new games. Thus, goes the argument, we need to strengthen and expand intellectual property rights to make up for the losses to come.

However, it would take only economics of a very sophomoric level to point out that changes like the Internet produce changes on both sides of the intellectual property scale. That is to say, the Internet makes copying easier. That might lead us to believe that we need to strengthen the rights of existing intellectual property holders to compensate for the loss that they might suffer because of the copying. But the Internet also, as any of you who have ever used a search engine would be able to testify, is probably the best copyright violation detection device ever invented. Those of you who are interested in MP3 music recordings, you may have noticed that there were stories initially about the MP3 files posted all over the Internet; copyrighted works posted illicitly by people who thought that it would just be fun to put up their favorite albums on the Internet. If you go and look for those now, out of a purely academic interest I'm sure, you will find that it is almost impossible to discover them. Why is that? Because the record companies can use the very same technologies, the facility of copying, in order to track down those people who have dot MP3 suffixes down there and to stop them. So at the very least we might want to ask: "Are the losses that the Internet is causing to intellectual property holders greater than, equal to, or less than the benefits that they are getting in terms of increased ability to track copyright violations, increased access to audience, decreased costs of distribution, and increased audience?"

The Changing Nature of Public Domain

In the 1960s, when a consumer made an audiocassette copy of a record for personal use, the economic consequences were seen as tolerable and its civic value was widely recognized. So, too, with individuals borrowing library books, making photocopies of newspaper articles or putting posters of rock stars on their dormitory room doors. But now that the Internet has created a new global communications infrastructure and marketplace, the criteria for determining the scope of the public domain are changing. Legitimate personal and non-commercial uses of copyrighted works that were once seen as isolated and trivial (or at least beyond the reach of the market and therefore moot) are being sharply curtailed. In asserting greater control over how their products may be used, copyright industries seek to criminalize the personal copying of CDs, the viewing of DVDs on unapproved electronic appliances and excerpting of digital material that in the print media would be considered fair use.

This is a new development: the dramatically changing character of the public domain in American society.

David Bollier, *Why the Public Domain Matters*, 2002.

The very short anecdote I would tell to illustrate this point is that of the video recorder. The video recorder was seen by Hollywood as a terrible thing—like the Internet—a new copying technology that would eat the heart out of Hollywood. Hollywood attempted first of all to lobby Congress to have VCRs and Sony Betamaxes taxed, then they tried to use the courts. Luckily for them, they lost both times. I say luckily because of course now Hollywood derives more than 50 percent of its revenues from the rental of videotapes. Here was a new copying technology that was seen only as a threat. "We need stronger intellectual property rights" comes the cry. Luckily, on that occasion neither Congress nor the courts were willing to aid the movie industry in its attempt to increase intellectual property rights and to make VCRs and videotapes more expensive. The sky did not fall. The new copying technology turned out to offer benefits as well as costs to the intellectual property owners. Conservatives have often enjoyed pointing out unintended consequences, and the need for caution in intervening in order to protect against supposed market failures. This story seems to me to be a classic case of both phenomena.

But it is not simply because Federalists wish to preserve constitutional limits on the power of Congress, and are skeptical about the need for state regulation of the market, that they should say that the recent expansions of intellectual property have gone too far. The Federalist society also professes a deep concern with individual liberty and an attachment to the "technologies of freedom," that empower the individual against the state. The Internet is surely such a technology. Yet the very features which make it so attractive as a technology of freedom, are the features that the intellectual property maximalists find so offensive. The "solutions" they propose, both legal and technical, are solutions that make the Net more centralized, more subject to state control, more zoned, and more regulated. From the point of view of the intellectual property maximalists, liberty "is a bug, not a feature." This is hardly a view that any good Federalist should subscribe to.

Periodical Bibliography

The following articles have been selected to supplement the diverse views presented in this chapter.

Glenn Otis Brown	"Running for Cover," *New Republic Online*, July 27, 2000, www.tnr.com.
Lisa Dean	"Q: Should Employers Have to Reveal Electronic Surveillance Activities? Yes: They Should Be Able to Guard Against Misuse of the Internet on Company Time," *Insight*, September 11, 2000.
Katherine Eban Finkelstein	"The Computer Cure: Privacy Isn't Always the Best Medicine," *New Republic*, September 14, 1998.
Christie Hefner, Michael Robertson, and Tyler Cowen	"New Technology and Intellectual Property," *CATO Policy Report*, January/February 2001.
Michael deCourcy Hinds	"Protecting Our Rights: What Goes on the Internet?" *National Issues Forums*, No. 189, 1998.
Issues and Controversies on File	"Internet Filtering Software," April 26, 2002.
Kenneth Jost	"Copyright and the Internet," *CQ Researcher*, September 29, 2000.
Jerry Kang	"Cyberspace Privacy: A Primer and Proposal," *Human Rights*, Winter 1999.
Daniel B. Klein	"Trust and Privacy on the Net," *Ideas on Liberty*, May 2000.
David Masci	"Internet Privacy," *CQ Researcher*, November 6, 1998.
Declan McCullagh	"Is Internet Privacy Overrated?" *Liberty*, August 1999.
Declan McCullagh	"Q: Should Employers Have to Reveal Electronic Surveillance Activities? No: It Is Not Good Business to Force Companies to Disclose Their Actions to Employees," *Insight*, September 11, 2000.
Joseph D. McNamara	"Big Brother Is Listening," *Hoover Digest*, No. 1, 1999.
Jeffrey Rosen	"Minor Infraction—The Supreme Court Misunderstands Porn," *New Republic*, June 3, 2002.
Erika Waak	"The Global Reach of Privacy Invasion," *Humanist*, November/December 2002.

CHAPTER 4

What Will Be the Future of the Information Revolution?

Chapter Preface

In the ever-evolving world of information technology, it often seems that computers and software programs that were considered cutting edge when they appeared on the market are obsolete soon after. Because technologies develop so rapidly, it can be difficult to determine which new tools will change society and which ones will end up in the discount bins. One promising technology is wearable computers, devices that users strap around their waists, wrists, or heads so that they can access and send data while keeping their hands free. The movement away from desktop and laptop computers may become central to the future of the Information Revolution.

These computers have already proven useful in manufacturing industries and the military. For example, technicians, operators, and others who do not work at a desk can use wearable computers during tasks such as inspections, inventories, and maintenance. In an article for *Science News*, Peter Weiss notes several ways in which the U.S. military is relying on these devices. According to Weiss, U.S. soldiers based in Bosnia have worn computers that can translate English into Serbo-Croatian, while Marines have tested a head-mounted display to aid in vehicle inspections.

While wearable computers are proving useful for many businesses and the armed forces, they have yet to break through into the personal market. However, there are people—"cyborgs" or "borgs"—who have chosen to spend their days connected to a computer. In his article, Weiss describes a typical outfit: a computer in a shoulder bag, a miniature computer display attached to a beret, and a keyboard strapped to the wearer's hand. According to Weiss, "To borgs . . . , wearing computers means adopting an entirely different lifestyle—a better lifestyle, borgs argue—in which the computer's always on and participating unobtrusively, often automatically, in nearly every facet of one's life. The enhanced self is continuously receiving information from anywhere in the world."

At present, these computers are not comfortable enough for most people to wear all day. The head-mounted displays can cause headaches and block vision while shoulder bags and keyboards can be awkward to carry. In response, some companies are developing fabrics that can conduct electricity so that people can actually wear computers while dressed in everyday clothing. One of these businesses, Santa Fe Science and Technology, announced in August 2002 that it had created conductive threads that can be woven into regular clothes and form wearable circuits and electronic devices. According to the online news source *Telecom Worldwire*, "Possible applications that the company has suggested include a shirt that monitors and responds to rises or falls in temperature, a pulse or blood pressure monitoring device for athletes or a cell phone that is integrated into an individual's shirt." Such clothing may be available by 2005.

The advent of wearable computers and other technologies that make it possible for people to use computers and the Internet regardless of location suggests that the Information Revolution has become a constant in the lives of many people throughout the world. In the following chapter, the authors evaluate whether or not emerging information technologies will benefit societies around the globe.

"The boundless credible expectations of the Internet will enhance our lives."

The Information Revolution Will Continue to Benefit Society

Joseph F. Coates

In the following viewpoint Joseph F. Coates asserts that the next two decades of the Information Revolution will bring forth a number of positive economic and social changes. According to Coates, the organizations and industries that will benefit from the ever-expanding Internet include retail stores, unions, and the health care industry. In addition, he contends that the Internet will increase entertainment and recreation options, make people safer, and allow for greater social interaction. Coates is the president of Consulting Futurist Inc. in Washington, D.C., and the coauthor of *2025: Scenarios of U.S. and Global Society Reshaped by Science and Technology*.

As you read, consider the following questions:
1. Other than the integration of media, what does Coates believe is the biggest thing affecting the Internet's future?
2. According to the author, how will the Internet benefit unionism?
3. In Coates's opinion, how will the Information Revolution change the practice of medicine?

Joseph F. Coates, "The Future of the Web," *The World & I*, vol. 17, April 2002, pp. 38–43. Copyright © 2002 by News World Communications, Inc. Reproduced by permission.

Through a series of scientific, technological, and business coincidences, the evolution of information technology has led to a disjointed, competitive, and piecemeal communications system.

The telegraph, telephone, and radio resulted from separate inventions, each converted into businesses by people with different objectives. Television came about as a spin-off from radio to compete with film. About 30 years ago the latest technological marvel, the Internet, was dropped into the middle of this communications chaos.

Unlike anything that came before, the Internet was free, or nearly so, in the minds of the early user. It featured video screens, computer keyboards, and communication to anyone, anywhere in the world, who was part of the Internet network. It has become increasingly sophisticated in quality and reliability, more convenient to use, and immeasurably more popular and valuable with the creation of the World Wide Web. Its democratic feature—open to anyone, anonymously, if you choose—was most appealing.

Major Changes Ahead

Looking ahead 15 to 20 years, the Internet will be unrecognizable. The rest of the telecommunications industry will also be unrecognizable as we approach the goal of universal, seamless communication from anyplace to anyplace, at any time.

Technological integration will be required through patchwork arrangements, either voluntarily or by government intervention. Businesses may evolve in an intelligent way to assume more and more of the total information package needed to serve all customers. AOL-Time Warner is taking a slow start in that direction.

On the technological side, the biggest thing affecting the future of the Internet, aside from the integration of media, is the emergence of wireless telecommunications. The new third-generation wireless service in the United States has enough broad-bandwidth capacity to service the Internet. Broadband means the capacity to speedily carry voice, text, photographs, graphics, movement, and interaction.

Wireless Internet will become as familiar as wireline Internet, with which it will be seamlessly integrated. Continually decreasing computer size, declining cost, and increasing numbers of users worldwide will define the total emerging system.

Existing applications are being substantially enhanced or expanded. Let's look at a number of these and see where they are going. Keep in mind that if costs drop as technology becomes more familiar and commonplace, it will expand the range of people, organizations, and institutions that will be on the system. As Internet pioneer Robert Metcalfe proposed years ago, the value of a network increases geometrically as the square of the number of people on the network.

Changing the Shopping Experience

Shopping by Internet is now widespread, in competition with catalog buying or visiting the mall. It is especially attractive where there is no shop, supplier, or boutique nearby. Despite exaggerated expectations, Internet shopping is enormously successful. As the quality of images and the capability of interaction grow, the Net will be the big challenge to catalogs, which derive their strength from small size, convenience, and use of color.

The Internet will allow you to see yourself, having sent a picture and your measurements to a vendor. If you are buying clothes, you will be able to examine a wide range of outfits, and place an order without ever leaving your chair, desk, or plane seat. You will be able to see yourself walking, sitting, or rotated at various angles in your outfits. (Some people will always want to shop traditionally because that is recreation for them.)

As with most new uses, it will not be either-or but will offer a widening of choices based on people's preferences and short-term pressures. Comparison shopping will be a cinch on the Internet and will drive down prices. Business-to-business network commerce is already flourishing and will expand tremendously. Auctions and various forms of bidding are already common and will become ubiquitous.

One consequence of Internet-based purchasing will be a radical change in logistics regarding the shipping of goods. As more things in smaller or larger packages are delivered to homes, offices, and business facilities, trucks themselves will change. The big ones will still be necessary, but there will be a lot more midsize and smaller ones to wend their way through the neighborhoods.

Some communities may resort to the Tokyo system, in which people place and pick up their Internet orders at a local chain, like 7-Eleven. The reason is that in Tokyo the street naming is so complex that it would be too expensive to deliver to individual addresses.

More Efficient Business Operations

Wireline and wireless will help business operate not only around the clock but around the world, in the sense that any element of the business personnel or unit can contact any other element, anytime and anywhere. Out of that capability will come enhanced efficiency and effectiveness, tighter management, or looser reins where that is appropriate.

There will be more interpersonal action between people who are now normally distant. Groupware, the ability of multiple locations to simultaneously communicate, exchange ideas, discuss matters, and work on projects, will be a cohesive factor in global business.

On the other hand, we will develop an etiquette that will be a constraint on who has the right to contact whom, when, for what purpose, and under what circumstances. After all, the system could easily drive everyone to a frazzle without proper protocol. Small businesses will benefit: the global Internet will allow any size enterprise to market worldwide and find (or be found by) members of niche markets.

The Internet Will Benefit Labor Unions

Some markets will shrivel and even wither away when it is cheaper, faster, and more reliable to do a task yourself. Examples include travel agents, financial service advisers, and automobile dealers. Their individual survival will depend on innovations in customer service.

Arthur Shostak, a longtime student of organized labor, foresees the emergence of cyber-unions. The Internet will not just improve the old tools of unionism but will open up new levels of excellence, making strategic planning more feasible, flexible, and practical. As unions gain international breadth, their actions will become more sophisticated.

In negotiations, if unions are able to call up the same in-depth information about the firm available to the employer, this will make solutions more mutually significant. The Internet will also allow unions to become more collegial, restoring the socialization and important interpersonal linkages that are so important to group cohesion and action.

Paralleling the new business-union relations will be public interest groups and non-governmental organizations dealing with national or international governing bodies. The ability to gather, collect, process, and deliver information in depth and on demand during a negotiation or discussion will change relationships. The ability to confront solid information with solid information will reduce hostile confrontations. In almost all interorganizational negotiations, the best route is establishing cooperation on as much common ground as possible.

Jobs of the Future

The hot new occupation/profession will be "new media professional" or "rich media professional." In the 1970s and 1980s, there was a great demand for "technical writers." In the 1990s, there was a great demand for "graphic artists." In the 2000s and beyond, there will be a great demand for "new media professionals." These people will have the skills of a videographer, an editor, a Web designer, a programmer, and an instructional designer. It's sort of like being a graphic designer/instructional designer for 4-D, online media. At a recent high-tech conference, every corporate executive in attendance wanted to hire anyone who could help stream video on the corporate network. Incidentally, the term "rich media" refers to a hybrid form of media in which the static information comes from, say, a CD-ROM disc; the dynamic media come from a high-speed hard drive, which provides the necessary buffering and assembly of media; and the up-to-the-minute information comes from one or more distant Web servers or databases.

Royal Van Horn, *Phi Delta Kappan*, June 2000.

Surveys and panel voting will be common. Most promising will be real-time voting during TV programs on individual characters, acts, sequences, and outcomes. The questionable judgments of those who manage the media may be replaced by the more practical and down-to-earth judgments of viewers.

People Will Be Safer

A surprisingly high percentage of people require supervision, whether as a condition of parole or for medical reasons. The availability of wireless-bandwidth capabilities will make it practical to have two-way audio, video, and data communication with them, ensuring that they remain law-abiding, safe, and healthy. The Internet will be able to identify where people are, remind them of what they must do—take a pill, exercise—and where they must go, and verify the safety of those who are at risk.

There will be a great deal more interaction through wireless Internet as the devices shrink in size and capacity grows. We might have wrist TVs, from the size of a wristwatch face up to anything that will be comfortable on your forearm.

The [September 11, 2001, terrorist attacks] have reminded all of us that oral communication is invaluable in an emergency. We will add to that the capability of imagery, which will be a primary improvement in dealing with physical, medical, social, occupational, or traffic emergencies. In a disaster, a picture will be invaluable in allocating resources, mobilizing, setting priorities, and managing rescue workers. . . .

A New Language

The Internet developed in the United States as if all the world spoke English and will do so forever. This is far from the truth, although English will be the dominant language for the English-speaking nations, most professionals, and big businesses.

Communications among multinational corporations and their principal suppliers will be in English. But when one gets down to the nitty-gritty, consumers' side of life, it seems unlikely that people who speak Turkish or Polish will search for and buy a washing machine using English rather than their native tongue.

A large expansion in new languages on the Internet is already under way. Keyboards will become more complex. In his book *Alpha Beta*, John Man points out that there is a universal Unicode, which stores 143 characters to represent the alphabets in all languages. Complex graphic languages such as Arabic will have keyboards that can be flipped back and forth between the local language and English.

The Chinese will use a Roman keyboard for email, using a script called Pinyin, which converts the sounds of Chinese into Roman letters. The system can even take into account the tonal differences that are so important in Chinese.

The lexicographer David Crystal claims that Netspeak is emerging as a third form of communication, the other two types presumably being speech and text. The Internet will steadily change our ideas of grammar, syntax, and vocabulary. With regard to it, RUOK [Are you okay]?

Other Ways the Internet Will Help People

Medicine is a favorite subject for discussions on the Internet now. New uses will offer a combination of speed and flexibility of response to an accident, disaster, or individual patients. The ability to incorporate broad-bandwidth imaging and interaction will allow the practitioner to examine and diagnose the patient at a distance. Routine data gathering and monitoring of patients will be transmitted to the physician's database.

A wireless Internet will transform sightseeing, eliminating the need to carry heavy guidebooks. It will allow you to call up anything you want, with the right level of detail to satisfy your needs.

You will not need to know the name of a building since GPS, the Global Positioning Satellite system, will automatically take care of that. The Internet will facilitate getting around in strange cities, minimizing the possibility of getting lost with no ready way of calling for help.

Transforming the Home

The Internet will be the core of the most important information-technology development in the home, the electronic home work-study center. It will bring together all of the information technologies connected with the house and all of their functions: work at home, entertainment, recreation, and socialization.

A typical home will have seven or eight flat screens. The

kitchen appliances will be connected to each other and networked to the Internet, allowing you to instruct them remotely from another room, your car, or your office. The ability to communicate internally with wireless will cost less than rewiring your house. Safety and security will cease to be concerns of the middle class and wealthy. The smart house will alert one to the presence of intruders, photograph them, and even capture them physically in many circumstances. The Internet will retain all the information it automatically sends to the police or fire department.

The Internet will allow you to participate remotely in celebrations, weddings, births, and funerals as you interact with other people through life-size wall screens. It will be the closest thing to being at the event, which may be 15 or 5,000 miles away.

The Internet will bring familiar forms of recreation into the home, but it will also lead to new types of entertainment and recreation. Socially, your contacts may be briefer but their numbers will be greater, and, on average, each will give satisfaction greater than you ever experienced before.

The boundless credible expectations of the Internet will enhance our lives, improve our work, free up our time, expand our contacts, and give most of us greater satisfaction in our activities.

"Even when everyone on the planet has been connected to the Internet, there will still be wars, and pollution, and inequality."

The Information Revolution Will Not Be a Panacea

Economist

Despite the claims of many "cybergurus," the Information Revolution cannot solve all of the world's problems, the *Economist* maintains in the following viewpoint. The magazine asserts that while the Internet has dramatically changed business practices and may help reduce inequality, it cannot end war and intolerance. In addition, the magazine argues that although some people believe that the Internet will reduce pollution, the increasing popularity of the Internet, and particularly online shopping, has in fact increased energy consumption. *Economist* is a weekly financial magazine.

As you read, consider the following questions:

1. What did Nicholas Negroponte claim, as stated by the magazine?
2. In the magazine's opinion, when is it more energy-efficient to do certain activities online?
3. According to *Economist*, why do poor people shun the Internet?

"It is impossible that old prejudices and hostilities should longer exist, while such an instrument has been created for the exchange of thought between all the nations of the earth." Thus Victorian enthusiasts, acclaiming the arrival in 1858 of the first transatlantic telegraph cable. People say that sort of thing about new technologies, even today. Biotechnology is said to be the cure for world hunger. The sequencing of the human genome will supposedly eradicate cancer and other diseases. The wildest optimism, though, has greeted the Internet. A whole industry of cybergurus has enthralled audiences (and made a fine living) with exuberant claims that the Internet will prevent wars, reduce pollution, and combat various forms of inequality. However, although the Internet is still young enough to inspire idealism, it has also been around long enough to test whether the prophets can be right.

Grandest of all the claims are those made by some of the savants at the Massachusetts Institute of Technology about the Internet's potential as a force for peace. One guru, Nicholas Negroponte, has declared that, thanks to the Internet, the children of the future "are not going to know what nationalism is." His colleague, Michael Dertouzos, has written that digital communications will bring "computer-aided peace" which "may help stave off future flare-ups of ethnic hatred and national break-ups." The idea is that improved communications will reduce misunderstandings and avert conflict. This is not new, alas, any more than were the claims for the peace-making possibilities of other new technologies. In the early years of the 20th century, aeroplanes were expected to end wars, by promoting international communication and (less credibly) by making armies obsolete, since they would be vulnerable to attack from the air. After the first world war had dispelled such notions, it was the turn of radio. "Nation shall speak peace unto nation," ran the fine motto of Britain's BBC World Service. Sadly, Rwanda's Radio Mille Collines disproved the idea that radio was an intrinsically pacific force once and for all.[1]

---

1. According to the United Nations, reports on the radio station helped incite the massacre of Rwanda's Tutsi rebels.

No Peace and Blue Skies

The mistake people make is to assume that wars are caused simply by the failure of different peoples to understand each other adequately. Indeed, even if that were true, the Internet can also be used to advocate conflict. Hate speech and intolerance flourish in its murkier corners, where governments . . . find it hard to intervene. Although the Internet undeniably fosters communication, it will not put an end to war. But might it reduce energy consumption and pollution? The Centre for Energy and Climate Solutions (CECS), a Washington think-tank, has advanced just such a case, based largely on energy consumption figures for 1997 and 1998. While the American economy grew by 9% over those two years, energy demand was almost unchanged—because, the CECS ventures, the Internet "can turn paper and CDs into electrons, and replace trucks with fibre-optic cable." No wonder one enthusiastic newspaper headline begged, "Shop online—save the earth."

Sadly, earth-saving is harder than that. Certainly, shopping online from home is far less polluting than driving to a shopping mall. Ordering groceries online, and having them delivered, means that, if the logistics are handled efficiently, one truck journey can replace dozens of families' separate car trips. Reading newspapers, magazines and other documents online is more efficient than printing and transporting them physically. Yet doing things online is more energy-efficient only if it genuinely displaces real-world activities. If people shop online as well as visiting the bricks-and-mortar store, the result is an overall increase in energy consumption. Thanks to the Internet, it is now easy for Europeans to order books and have them extravagantly air-freighted from America before they are available in Europe. And it is more efficient to read documents online only if doing so replaces, rather than adds to, the amount of printed [material].

Furthermore, as more and more offices and homes connect to the Internet, millions of PCs, printers, servers and other devices gobble significant quantities of energy. Home computers are becoming part of the fabric of everyday life, and are increasingly left switched on all the time. One controversial assessment concluded that fully 8% of electricity consumption in America is due to Internet-connected computers. The construction of vast "server farms"—warehouses full of computers and their attendant cooling systems—has contributed to the overloading of the electrical power network that has caused brown-outs in Silicon Valley.

Inequality Might Be Reduced

What about the belief that the Internet will reduce inequality? According to a study carried out by America's Department of Commerce, households with annual incomes above $75,000 are more than 20 times as likely to have Internet access as the poorest households. [Former president] Bill Clinton, struck by the "digital divide" between rich and poor, argue[d] that universal Internet access would help to reduce income inequality.

Bateman. © 2000 by Scott Bateman. Reprinted by permission of North America Syndicate.

But, as the cost of using the Internet continues to fall (services offering free access are becoming the norm, and a basic PC can now be had for little more than a video recorder or a large television), the true reason for the digital divide between rich and poor will become apparent. The poor are not shunning the Internet because they cannot afford it: the problem is that they lack the skills to exploit it effectively. So it is difficult to see how connecting the poor to the Internet will improve their finances. It would make more sense to aim for universal literacy than universal Internet access. Yet, even in the more ludicrous claims for the Internet, there may be germs of truth. This open network, so hard for governments to control, may indeed help to give more power to individual citizens and encourage democracies. As democratic governments rarely fight each other, that might promote peace. As for the environment, the Internet will allow many pieces of machinery to be monitored and tuned more precisely from afar. That will promote energy efficiency. Taxing or merely measuring pollution will be less expensive and so easier for governments to undertake.

Even inequality may, in some cases, be reduced thanks to the Internet. A computer programmer in Bangalore or Siberia can use the Internet to work for a software company in Seattle without leaving home, and can expect to be paid a wage that is closer to that of his virtual colleagues at the other end of the cable. The effect is not to reduce income inequality between people doing similar jobs in different countries, but to increase the inequality between information workers in poor countries and their poorest compatriots.

The Internet changes many things. It has had a dramatic impact on the world of business. Firms can now link their systems directly to those of their suppliers and partners, can do business online around the clock, and can learn more than ever about their customers. Economies may be more productive as a result. For individuals, e-mail has emerged as the most important new form of personal communication since the invention of the telephone.

The Limits of Technology

The extent to which the Internet will transform other fields of human endeavour, however, is less certain. Even when everyone on the planet has been connected to the Internet, there will still be wars, and pollution, and inequality. As new gizmos come and go, human nature seems to remain stubbornly unchanged; despite the claims of the techno-prophets, humanity cannot simply invent away its failings. The Internet is not the first technology to have been hailed as a panacea—and it will certainly not be the last.

"[Information and communication technologies] can make a real difference in the lives of the poor."

The Information Revolution Will Benefit Developing Nations

David Morrison

In the following viewpoint David Morrison asserts that information and communication technologies (ICTs) benefit impoverished nations in three important ways. According to Morrison, intelligent use of ICTs can greatly improve the quality of health care and education in developing nations. In addition, he argues that these technologies create jobs and boost productivity while also increasing global awareness of the problems faced by the poor. Morrison is the president of Netaid.org Foundation, an organization that uses the Internet to help fight poverty.

As you read, consider the following questions:

1. In the author's view, how would the creation of efficient online marketplaces improve the development industry?
2. How does the Grameen Phone program increase productivity, according to the author?
3. According to Morrison, what is the source of ICTs' power?

David Morrison, "An Outlet to Growth," *WorldLink*, vol. 14, September/October 2001. Copyright © 2001 by Global Agenda, the magazine of the World Economic Forum Annual Meeting. Reproduced by permission.

C an the Internet be used to alleviate poverty? [In 2000] this seemed a sure bet. At the height of the dotcom boom the Internet and other new communications technologies were seen by many to hold revolutionary new potential for making people less poor by bringing to them the full benefits of the information revolution. In many cases the so-called leapfrogging technologies, such as cellular telephones, would allow poor countries to bypass the costly introduction of more traditional means of communications, such as landline telephones, and accelerate social and economic development. Turning the digital divide into a digital opportunity for poor countries was a major theme of the G8 summit in Okinawa in July 2000, where the Japanese government announced a major fund for technology and poverty initiatives, and the G8 created a public sector–private sector Digital Opportunities Task Force (DOT Force) to address the issue.

Reappraising the Power of the Internet

The world looks different little more than a year later. There were of course sceptics all along: at a major conference in Seattle on "creating digital dividends" in the fall of 2000, Bill Gates poured cold water on the notion that information and communication technologies (ICTs) could or should be used to fight poverty. "Do people have a clear view of what it means to live on $1 a day?" Gates asked, before arguing that investments in human rights, health and education made much more sense for poor countries than investments in ICTs. The dotcom crash has led to an overall reappraisal of what the Internet can and cannot do. And new questions about the costs and likelihood of rapid adoption of third-generation wireless telecommunications make the early extension of networks to include the world's poor, especially in rural areas, far from certain. Tellingly, at the . . . G8 summit in Genoa, digital-divide issues received scant attention by political leaders and the press.

Is the notion of using ICTs to fight poverty simply the latest victim of the burst technology bubble? Certainly Gates's sobering analysis, near the height of the hype, struck many as simply common sense: cell phones and laptops are not obvious priorities for communities that do not have clean water, or are struggling to cope with HIV/Aids. Yet the poverty-fighting potential of ICTs should not be written off so abruptly. Even if the notion of "a PC in every hut" makes little sense, ICTs still show considerable promise for making people less poor in at least three major ways.

Improving the Development Industry

First, retooling the existing development industry, including putting some of its key processes online, would lead to strong efficiency gains, leaving more money to combat poverty directly. Flows of official development assistance (ODA) from rich to poor countries currently stand at roughly $40 billion per year. Money channelled through private groups, such as churches and nongovernmental organizations (NGOs), adds several billion to this figure. The overall industry, however, is fragmented and inefficient, with overlap and duplication in some areas and unmet needs in others. This is partly a result of politicisation (donors like to control where their money goes), but much could be done through the creation of efficient online marketplaces, which would help to rationalise the industry, make it more transparent and reduce transaction costs. Several commercial initiatives in this direction have begun, but it is too early to tell what impact they will have.

Second, at the downstream end, better use of information technology would allow recipient countries to coordinate inflows of aid much more effectively (a country the size of Kenya may be host to 50–100 different aid agencies, often with little effective coordination among them, despite efforts of the UN and the World Bank). And better use of information technology for knowledge management would help to ensure, for example, that an effective programme of decentralisation of state services that was highly beneficial to the poor in one country could more quickly become known and replicated in another. Again, there have been several steps in the right direction, but knowledge management by the major industry players, such as the UN and World Bank, is still rudimentary, especially when compared with global companies in the private sector. A much more ambitious attempt at online sharing of knowledge and best practice throughout the international development community, the World Bank–sponsored "Development Gateway", has yet to take off.

Connecting the World's Poor

Despite the bursting of the bubble, the poverty alleviating potential of directly connecting the world's poor remains real. The challenges are great: Sao Paulo, Brazil, has more international bandwidth than all of Africa, and barely 6% of the world's people are Internet users, while over half of humanity has never made a telephone call. On the face of it, the choice between clean water and computers is not much of a choice at all. Yet, "clean water or computers" is a false dichotomy—ICTs should be seen as a tool to help meet existing development objectives rather than as a stand-alone sector.

ICTs show particular promise in enabling poor countries to make real progress in the health and education sectors. Consider the power of distance learning for overcoming two root causes of poverty, ignorance and isolation. The world's knowledge is now available in ways unimaginable before the advent of the Internet, and it is increasingly reaching developing countries via telecentres and other commercial or government-sponsored points of community access in countries such as Egypt, Turkey and the Dominican Republic. In Jordan, King Abdullah II, making good on his Davos 2000 [the World Economic Forum 2000 in Davos, Switzerland] commitment to shrink the digital divide in his country, is spearheading a programme to build 1,000 Internet-connected centres in poor areas within the next five years. According to the United Nations Development Programme (UNDP), the first of these to open are already oversubscribed by people taking formal classes, exchanging email with contacts in other cities, researching issues such as health and religion and exploring business opportunities. In many countries such centres are a boon to women in particular, who often face cultural and other barriers to travelling far from home in search of learning opportunities. While bringing relevant knowledge "the last mile" beyond communal points of access to extremely poor rural areas still presents challenges, innovative solutions, such as simply broadcasting via radio relevant material found on the Internet, are being found.

In the health sector, where knowledge is often the best remedy for fighting disease, the potential of ICTs is equally strong. They can be used by healthcare professionals to acquire information on the spread of disease and to disseminate knowledge about how to combat it. As early as 1993, an international programme supported by the UN and the World Bank linked 11 developing countries to medical databases in developed countries, and to each other, by satellite technologies. More recently, in the Gambia the Internet has been used to conduct long-distance medical diagnoses, and across sub-Saharan Africa it has been used to monitor the spread of meningitis and to coordinate vaccination programmes in response. . . .

The Economic Benefits of Information Technology

Developing countries are much more likely to use information technology to access ideas than to generate them. The main benefits of information technology in a developing country will be access to information and communications. Improvements in the productivity of the service sector are likely to be smaller than in developed countries because of the lack of complementary inputs. Information technology requires a highly trained workforce, which developing countries lack.

One consequence of this is that developed countries will gain a comparative advantage in tradable services. The comparative advantage of developing countries is likely to remain in raw materials and manufacturing using "old", easily mastered, technologies. Increasing imports of services from the developed world may actually bring benefits to developing countries if these information-rich services can be used to increase efficiency in the production, or marketing, of manufactured products.

David Canning, "Telecommunications, Information Technology and Economic Development," December 1999.

In the business sector, ICTs help to create and sustain networks that produce one of the greatest weapons against poverty—new jobs. Perhaps the most striking example is that of Grameen Phone in Bangladesh. The model is simple. Grameen lends rural entrepreneurs (usually women) the money to purchase mobile telephones, which operate via a network in which Grameen is a part owner. The entrepreneurs become village-level resellers of telephone calls, earning a respectable income for themselves and enabling their communities to communicate with one another. This communication, in turn, helps to create social and economic networks that lead to better decision-making and increased productivity. For instance, farmers can make informed decisions about where and when to sell their produce, and deals can be struck over distances. The same effect is being felt in India and China, where mobile services are flourishing, in part because mobile phones are becoming a sound business investment, even for the poor.

The best technologies have poverty-fighting potential across a number of sectors. A fast-growing US company called Voxiva has developed a new technology that in effect gives anyone with access to a telephone, fixed or mobile, the equivalent of an interactive voicemail account through which they can access a range of network-specific applications. The Peruvian Ministry of Health, an early client, is using this technology to allow rural health workers to report diseases, check lab results and send and receive messages in real time. At the same time, clients in the commercial sector can communicate and transact effectively and cheaply with their dispersed employees and customers (imagine the productivity gain of small business owners simply punching in their orders over the telephone—any telephone—instead of hoping the supplier's truck brings what they need the next time it calls). For Voxiva, the key has been developing a technology that promises many of the same benefits as Internet-based business-to-business commerce, but does so by using a device that is much more accessible to the poor in many developing countries—the telephone.

The Internet Can Mobilize People

In the end, the real power of ICTs stems from the network effects they help to create whether in health, education or any other poverty-fighting sector. Studies [in 1991] by the G8's DOT Force and others point to a number of key areas for action in developing countries if this network effect is to take hold. . . . Countries like Brazil, Estonia, Malaysia and

South Africa are seeing the benefits of their investment and commitment to ICTs. It remains true, however, that for many developing countries, particularly the poorest ones that attract little attention from the international private sector, real progress is years away.

This does not mean that countries with little immediate prospect of becoming fully connected will be left out entirely. There is a third, less direct but still potentially powerful way in which the global ICT revolution can affect the lives of those living in poverty: From the flurry of short text messages that helped bring down Filipino president Joseph Estrada, to the campaigns to ban landmines and drop the debt, to the protests at Seattle and Genoa, ICTs have become a tool for mass mobilisation and action. They have made the world smaller and more transparent, which has helped draw attention to the plight of the poor. Internet-enabled global networks have also made direct action more possible. Some of the most innovative uses of ICTs have occurred spontaneously in response to natural disasters: answers to an emergency appeal over the Internet by a Honduran NGO in the wake of Hurricane Mitch in 1998 were received within four hours. In the aftermath of the earthquake in Gujarat, India, earlier [in 1991], the Internet was used to collect funds (including from the Indian population in Silicon Valley), transmit information and solicit volunteers. In both cases, ICTs helped to bring the reality of what was happening on the ground to the wider world, in real time, and to facilitate an immediate response. . . .

For developing countries any choice between clean water and computers is clear. But this view of the role of ICTs in fighting poverty is too narrow. By helping to rationalise the existing development business, by helping to bring the benefits of the information revolution directly to the poor in developing countries and by facilitating the mobilisation of support for the fight against poverty around the world, ICTs can make a real difference in the lives of the poor. They are not a panacea. But they are effective new tools to enable the exchange of information and ideas which, in turn, help to build the social and economic networks that lead to real advances in development.

> *"All the gigabytes of information whizzing around the world in nano-seconds is not necessarily spreading knowledge."*

The Information Revolution Will Not Benefit Developing Nations

Kunda Dixit

Developing nations should not rely on information technology to solve their economic and social problems, Kunda Dixit claims in the following viewpoint. According to Dixit, information technology is far too expensive for people in developed countries to purchase and use, a situation that will likely persist well into the future. Dixit also argues that the information available on the Internet is not necessarily truthful or beneficial. He asserts that rather than investing in computers and software, nations such as Nepal and Pakistan should focus on the education and health care needs of their citizens. Dixit is a journalist from Nepal.

As you read, consider the following questions:
1. What is Bill Gates's view on the role of the Internet in the developing world, as cited by Dixit?
2. According to the author, what percentage of the world's population has ever logged on to the Internet?
3. How have developing countries failed to use shortwave radio properly, in Dixit's view?

It is a bit of an irony isn't it that those of us who are most sceptical about the potential for new information technologies to somehow leapfrog development are the ones who use this technology most intensively. Here we are writing about why a computer attached to a phone line is not the panacea it is made out to be to solve problems of poverty, and these very words are inputted into a computer and transmitted along a phone line to the newsroom.

Technology Is Not a Cure-All

Not all cybersceptics are Luddites [people opposed to technological advances]. The questions we have about information technology also apply to previous technological breakthroughs which we were told would save the earth. We are so desperate to find a clean, quick solution to the problems of poverty, the ecological crisis, the growing gap between rich and poor between and within countries, war and social injustice that we will jump at anything that offers a glimmer of hope. We are conditioned to look for technological fixes. Technology is easy, it is something you can lay your hands on, you buy it and the problem is fixed. But many of Nepal's problems are political, economic, socio-cultural. They demand complicated and sequenced interventions, the outcome is often unforeseen and messy, and the process of change will be slow.

After a decade of bonanza, the massive power of dotcom startups to generate cash, and the hype, we now seem to be settling down to a more sober assessment of the limitations of information technology. Even the *Economist* carried a cover earlier [in 2001] with the strapline: "What the Internet Cannot Do"—and they were not even talking about the Third World. Bill Gates is the latest unlikely cybersceptic: at an IT conference in November 2000 in Redmond, Washington, he spoke passionately about how the Internet was not any use to the world's poor. Said Gates: "The world's poorest two billion people desperately need health care, not laptops, or wireless Internet connections or a bridge across the digital divide." Many people couldn't believe that the guru of the cyberage was having doubts.

We haven't escaped the hype in our own region. India's Minister of Information Technology, Pramod Mahajan, has given up his homespun cotton shirt for a smart suit and a slick tie. He says India missed the bus on the industrial revolution, it can no longer afford to do the same with the information revolution. He wants to take his country from the potato chip to microchip, and the country has seen investments in the software industry double [since 2000]. But how is a country in which only 0.5 percent of the population has a PC, and less than three percent have phones, and where six-hour power cuts are commonplace, leapfrog? The joke is that 95 percent of Indians are waiting for phones, the other five percent are waiting for dial tones. All of South Asia is struggling to solve infrastructure bottlenecks, but it is a question of priorities. What is more important at the present time: a high-speed data trunk line or a network bringing safe drinking water to villages? The 700 million South Asians who live below the poverty line, the 53 percent of children who are malnourished, do not make the headlines. And yet the question we must ask is: how are the few thousand well-educated cyber-savvy South Asians going to make a difference to the billion compatriots who are not so fortunate?

South Asia is a land of contrasts. Despite infrastructure problems, most of the software engineers and programmers in Silicon Valley are from South Asia, and India's low-cost English-speaking young people with good education have firmly hitched their wagons to the information revolution. Sri Lanka, Bangladesh and even Nepal are leaping on to the business of data inputting across continents.

The Internet is supposed to level the playing field and make information freely available to everyone. There is a basic fallacy here: the Internet cannot do that simply because it is priced way beyond the reach of even the middle class. Only five percent of the world's 6.2 billion people have ever logged on, and nine out of ten in industrialised countries. A computer costs one fourth of the monthly household income of an average Finn, whereas it represents ten years' earnings for an average Nepali. It is not surprising therefore that one in every three Americans uses the Internet, but only one in every 10,000 people in India, Pakistan and Bangladesh do.

No doubt, there is a need to level the playing field. But with a digital divide like that, information technology is not going

174

Underprivileged and Dispossessed

There is no single digital divide but lots of overlapping ones: between old and young, men and women, rich and poor, blacks and whites, northern hemisphere and southern hemisphere and, above all, between developed and developing nations.

This is the area where the creation of a vast new underprivileged digitariat, even more dispossessed than now seems inevitable unless dramatic action is taken.

The bald statistics are depressingly familiar: barely 2% of the world's population of more than [six billion] are linked to the internet; most people on the planet have not even made a telephone call, let alone accessed the web; there are more telephone lines in a big city like Tokyo than in the whole of sub-Saharan Africa. In the US, internet access costs a user only 1% of average monthly income, whereas in Uganda it costs more than a month's average (per capita) income.

Victor Keegan, *Guardian*, December 14, 2000.

to do it for us. There is now a whole industry that is growing around the self-perpetuating world of development aid, which puts information technology forward as the panacea where all else has failed. The argument goes: the global gap between those with access to information technology and those without is growing, therefore the only way to catch up is to buy people computers and hook them up to the Internet.

Using Technology Properly

The other problem with presenting the Internet as the answer to all our ills is the belief that information will set us free. All the gigabytes of information whizzing around the world in nano-seconds is not necessarily spreading knowledge. Even if the Internet were distributing information widely and cheaply, what results is not necessarily greater wisdom. For information to be useful, it has to get to where it is needed as cheaply as possible, it needs to be relevant to the daily needs of the people it is meant for, and the information must be packaged so that it is easily understood. Information must help people communicate and participate, and allow them and their rulers to make informed choices. It must be affordable, it must make sense, and it must be user-friendly. Otherwise it is just junk mail. It is background radiation of inane digital trivia whizzing about at the speed of light. The other question to ask about information is whether there are any filters: who produces it, who controls it, who benefits? Technology is never value-free.

We tend to get all worked up about information technology, we are dazzled by the latest gadgets, gizmos and its glamorous manifestation. It's a bit like the automobile industry: whose car looks sleekest, whose is fastest, who's got the biggest hard-drives?

What all the talk of convergence eclipses is that a good, old-fashioned shortwave radio is also information technology. Developing countries that have completely wasted the power of radio to spread information and to communicate have no right to go on about "leapfrogging" into the Internet age. Our born-again digirati may snobbishly wave away AM radio, but no other medium in Nepal today comes close to matching the reach, the accessibility and affordability of shortwave radio. If there is one medium that will do all the things we want the Internet to do in Nepal (spread knowledge to the disadvantaged, make useful everyday information available to them) then radio is it.

And yet, what have we done with radio? We have used it shamelessly as a public address system for government propaganda, we have insulted the nine million or so radio listeners in Nepal by making shortwave and medium wave broadcasts so boring that people listen to it only because there is little else on the airwaves in Nepali. Radio, in fact, has become a symbol of official neglect and proof of an unspoken strategy to deny the weak a voice. If the information superhighway is full of potholes, an ox cart may be more suitable than a Sports Utility Vehicle.

Then, take education. How is the Internet going to help us leapfrog in education if we have made such a mess of our existing school system? Before sticking a computer into a school, how about building a roof over it? Why not first ensure children are properly fed? Provide textbooks? These things need to be fixed first, but the mechanism by which important political and economic decisions are made has not changed, decision-making is in the same hands, value-systems are the same. It is doubtful that the Internet can do it for us.

"[America's] ability to compete internationally in the innovation arena is crucial."

The Information Revolution Will Become More Competitive

Nicholas Imparato

In the following viewpoint Nicholas Imparato argues that the United States risks losing its position as the leader of the Information Revolution because other nations have become more innovative. He contends that South Asian and European nations have been able to expand their research and development of information technology while keeping costs low. According to Imparato, the United States will not remain at the front of the Information Revolution unless the business, university, and government communities work together to determine the best ways to develop, teach, and utilize new technologies. Imparato is a professor of marketing and management at the McLaren School of Business at the University of San Francisco and a research fellow at the Hoover Institution, a public policy research center that evaluates the causes and consequences of social, political, and economic change.

As you read, consider the following questions:
1. By how much has South Korea increased its patents since 1982, as cited by the author?
2. According to Imparato, what are some of the innovations that relied on federal support?
3. According to the author, which factors can help speed up the innovation process?

Innovation has become the operative word in business. From reengineering to corporate transformation to product "Web-izing," the idea is the same: finding ways to make money with a new product, service, or process. Now, however, warnings about the sustainability of U.S. innovation leadership appear.

America Is Facing New Challenges

A book published [in 1998] by the Council on Competitiveness in Washington, D.C., *Going Global: The New Shape of American Innovation*, details the weaknesses emerging in the national platform that supports innovation across industry sectors. The book grew out of an unprecedented study with more than 100 research and development leaders at companies, universities, and laboratories representing over $70 billion in research and development (R&D) investments. As the council's Debra van Opstal put it, "The danger is that the unique set of conditions that have propelled the United States to a position of world leadership over the last 50 years is not sufficient to keep us there for the next 50 years." The concerns are particularly sharp in the information technology sector.

William Hambrecht, legendary venture investor associated with Adobe Systems Inc., Genentech Inc., and Sybase, phrased the threat succinctly: "The competitive challenge for the future is likely to come not just from low-cost producers, but from low-cost innovators." For example, South Korea had a negligible position in the U.S. patent system in 1982 but has increased its patents by 40,000 percent since then. Now it is ahead of the United Kingdom and is coming up close behind Germany. Taiwan has increased its presence by 8,000 percent during the same time period. India's highly regarded technical university system and low labor costs for programmers are promoting the country's position as a technology center. Ireland's incentives for the manufacturing sector have expanded to R&D. In effect, the "innovation club" is growing. The movement of IT (information technology) manufacturing offshore—often promoted with tax incentives and subsidies—is challenging. The manufacturing sector accounts for 73 percent of business research. The concern is that as manufacturing moves offshore, important, fundamental research pursued in the United States will diminish. In addition, the tendency to colocate certain types of research with manufacturing will also negatively affect the sustainability of design superiority in electronics and software. Although world trade in IT products and services is growing, the U.S. trade deficit in IT has increased for most of [the 1990s].

An Unprepared Educational System

Just as the second industrial revolution displacing steam power required a mechanically literate workforce, so the American economy of the early 21st century will require a computer- and communications-literate workforce. It will need inventors and innovators to push out the envelope of the possible in the use of these technologies. It will need engineers and technicians to staff the industries—and to manage the interfaces between information technology and the rest of the economy. It will need a public with sufficient knowledge to use the great network and its computers productively.

Our educational system does not seem up to the task. One consequence of increasing income inequality in America in the past quarter-century has been a decline in effective political support for public services that are paid for by the rich and used by all. By the same token, we seem indifferent to the possibilities of recruiting talent abroad.

Stephen S. Cohen, J. Bradford DeLong and John Zysman, *Milken Institute Review*, First Quarter 2000.

Furthermore, federal funding drove a great deal of long-term, frontier research in the past. Since the 1980s, however, the government has been disinvesting in all forms of research and development. The significance of this trend is striking when you look at a list of innovations that depended on federal support: Networking, computer graphics, parallel computing, and windows and mouse user interfaces are among those the council noted as major advances dependent on government investment.

Learning New Technologies

How do we deal with the fact that the competition is getting better? According to Maurice Holmes, chief engineer of Xerox Corp., the only way we can obtain competitive advantage is by using our advantage in information technology to "learn faster than the rest of the world." Fast information diffusion through extended enterprises, strategic alliances, and public-private partnerships turbocharge the innovation process.

Holmes notes that innovation is occurring so quickly in hardware, software, and process that both the IT workforce and consumers face an increasingly difficult task in absorbing successive generations of technology. The ability to leverage information networks to diffuse information quickly and educate employees and consumers is one of the keys to success—both for companies and national economies.

We know little about how to use information technology to increase learning rates and even less about how people learn. As just one data point: Less than one tenth of a percent of the nation's educational expenditures in grades K-12 is devoted to understanding what actually works in education, observed David Shaw, chairman and CEO of D.E. Shaw, in the council's report. And no one has sufficiently explored the use of information technology to expand learning potential at any educational level. At the same time, we need to address the threats offshore enterprises pose, by creating an innovation-friendly regulatory environment. The permitted pace of IT write-offs, for example, often does not match reality. Our research system needs to be strengthened; our efforts at protecting intellectual property, both domestically and internationally, need to be redoubled. And so on. There is much to do.

Whether viewed in terms of high-wage jobs, national security, or economic vitality, our ability to compete internationally in the innovation arena is crucial. This goal is too important to be left to an innovation elite, but should engage the efforts of the wider business, government, and university communities.

"The world is smaller, the barriers between us are theoretically shrinking, and our potential to build a truly international movement is great."

The Internet Could Help Build a Global Democracy

Andrew Hammer

In the following viewpoint Andrew Hammer contends that the Internet has made it easier for people to publish and debate ideas and may eventually foster democracy worldwide. However, he argues that such a major advancement will not occur unless the online presence of women, poor people, and blue-collar workers is increased. He also maintains that members of online political organizations should avoid becoming isolated from the concerns of the real world. Hammer is the secretary general for the International League of Religious Socialists and the chair of the International Committee of the Democratic Socialists of America.

As you read, consider the following questions:
1. What are online campaigns, as explained by Hammer?
2. According to the author, what has the American left historically lacked?
3. According to Hammer, what has replaced mentoring and the gaining of knowledge through life experiences?

Andrew Hammer, "Talkin' About a Revolution: How Being Online Has Changed Our Lives," *Democratic Left*, vol. 27, 1999, pp. 27–28. Copyright © 1999 by *Democratic Left*. Reproduced by permission.

In the past ten years, the Internet has gone from being a novel invention used by universities, scientists, government agencies, and a few people in the know, to a center of communication, ideas, and commerce now used [by] millions round the globe. Part library, part television, the World Wide Web (WWW, or 'the Web'—a graphically-based multimedia method of providing information through the Internet) has made it possible for anyone interested in anything to simply enter a word into a search page, and find something somewhere on the Internet that addresses that topic.

For the socialist movement, the WWW has in some ways been the greatest equalizer we have ever had, in that our ideas are made as accessible to the public as major news outlets. But as with any new technological development, there are both light and dark sides to the Internet's entry into our lives.

Ideas Are More Accessible

The ability of the Web to make information available without regard to time or space has meant that anyone with an idea can publish it and put it in front of our faces just as easily as corporations and major media outlets. The obvious benefit of this for socialists and others on the left is that we are finally able to break out of the financial constraints on our ability to reach the public by conventional means (printing costs, broadcast and print media access, travel, etc.), and can now reach millions from one computer to another. The accessibility of an idea no longer hinges on what CNN or *The New York Times* will tell us, or what books and publications our libraries and shops choose (or more significantly for our movement, don't choose) to stock. In the online world, CNN and Democratic Socialists of America (DSA) both come over the same phone lines and use the same computer screen, and ultimately we are all looking at the same glowing box in our offices and homes. The difference is that we program this network ourselves.

At the same time, the use of e-mail means that communication about those ideas can occur between people in a way that has never before been possible. The creation of the online campaign, in which people use Web-based petitions, e-mail lists, and e-mail letter-writing campaigns to raise awareness about a particular issue, has allowed people to participate in political activism instantaneously from anywhere on the planet. While it's more common to have an ongoing political campaign brought onto the Internet, the past few years have seen campaigns on issues originated online, such as the Free Burma Coalition. In the case of the Jubilee 2000 campaign to relieve world debt, the Web was used to expand the movement by helping to create new international branches of a movement that had started out in Britain.

Yet more important is the ability not only to discover and join in with existing ideas, but to use the Internet to participate in the creation of new ones. It is now possible for some-one in New York and someone in New Zealand to have a daily correspondence, or even a real-time written discussion, on the drafting of a political document. E-mail lists (which connect any number of users to the same string of messages through one central address) and chat rooms abound, where issues of the day as well as the politics of particular organi-zations are discussed and debated.

The Beginnings of a New Democracy

The fact that so many people are now connected, with far more to connect in the future, has given rise to the idea of online democracy, where people are actually able to vote through their computer. That's crucial in more ways than one, because along with ideas, and the ability to shape them, comes the accessibility *to* those ideas by people who may have felt excluded in the past. People with disabilities who may find it difficult to have their ideas heard in a traditional setting, elderly people who find travel difficult, or simply people whose lives or income level make it difficult to attend face-to-face meetings or public forums are now enabled to take a seat at the discussion table through online forums.

As we cross over into a new century, we may have achieved the faint beginnings of a form of democracy that heretofore was only imagined by science fiction writers. The world is smaller, the barriers between us are theoretically shrinking, and our potential to build a truly international movement is great. But before we get too carried away with all of the wonderful things this new technology can do, let's take a look at some of the problems we've already encountered.

Internet Imperfection

While lower prices and aggressive programs by both business and governments have worked to make computers more available to the masses, most people in the world remain offline. Of those who are online, the demographic is still predominately middle to upper class males in industrialized nations. To be sure, there are thousands of people actively using the Internet in Bolivia, Azerbaijan, and Ghana, but the concern that the Internet excludes developing nations is certainly valid. And even within nations that are highly connected to the Net, class, gender and race are issues that have to be considered when we start talking about how great it is that "everyone" is online. They're not, and you can be assured that this [viewpoint] is not the only place where you will read about the danger of a brave new online world of creativity, conversation, and commerce that leaves out millions of working and poor people.

And women. They are going online in increasing numbers, but that brings us to another issue regarding how the Internet has worked in practice as opposed to the ideal. As I mentioned above, the text of an e-mail list takes away all of the physical characteristics by which we would normally judge the various authors of messages. But what it does not take away is the socialization of men and women into roles given to us long ago. Many of us have seen the television studies of classrooms that show boys constantly raising their hands to answer questions (even when they're not sure they know the answer), while the girls wait to be called upon. Unfortunately, the Internet hasn't changed that at all, and it's not likely to as long as so many of the men online continue to feel that each one of their many contributions is essential reading for us all. To their credit, women have sought out and created places online where they can exchange ideas among themselves, much as they have had to do in the real world. However, the goal for those of us online should be to check the way we are communicating, to make sure that there is the more important human dimension.

Internet Use and Political Affiliation

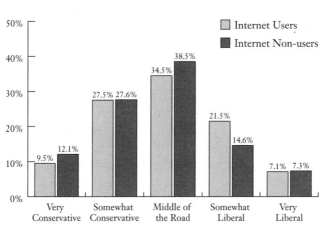

UCLA Center for Communication Policy, *The UCLA Internet Report: Surveying the Digital Future*, 2001.

Not far from that problem is one that affects not only our movement, but all organizations that involve some sort of appeal to their members and the general public. The level of discourse on the Net is so quick, so fascinating, that it becomes very easy for political activists of all stripes to develop and attach a false sense of meaning to their online communications. We in the American left are well aware that we have historically lacked a significant base in our communities—that is, any kind of real day to day political involvement with the people we claim to represent. The danger is that for some of us, the Internet has become a substitute for that face to face action in the community. Those who are more comfortable venting their brain on a screen (where they are ensconced in a virtual, Platonic "round table" of intellects) than they are dealing with real live working people, run the risk of getting lost in a sea of online pontificating that becomes an ivory moat around the proverbial ivory tower. The virtual community replaces the actual one, talk itself becomes a substitute for action, and people see their online musings as accomplishments when they are really nothing more than parts of the same ongoing conversation we always seem to carry on among ourselves.

Democratizing the Internet

Across the political spectrum, we have seen online communities spring up where a particular group of people around one organization begin talking about that organization, drafting policy, and making decisions without even realising that 50 people engaged in an online forum is not the organization, and is not properly representative of that organization. The result is that the number of active participants in an already small organization is shrunk even more by what becomes an *online ghetto* composed only of those who have computers, spend a great deal of time online, and have either the stamina or stubbornness to argue endlessly amongst themselves about the minutiae of their organization. The larger issues, the whole membership, and the community we advocate for are left behind for the sake of the cyber-jockies, who may not even be members of the organization the forum is based upon. Things like mentoring, and the acquisition of knowledge in the context of life experience, are often replaced by naked opinion derived from sweet-sounding documents of position and principle not based in any real social practice. The problem is that for better or worse, none of this contemplating and philosophising makes it out into the real world, and even [when] it does, words alone do not translate themselves into actions. It's *people* who do the translating. So while the Internet does provide us a marvelous opportunity to reach out to the world around us like never before, we have to guard against becoming so absorbed in the community online that we disappear from the other community; the one that supplies the phone lines and electricity, as well as water, underfunded transport and education, and almost no health care except for those lucky enough to have insurance. More than the telephone or radio or television, the personal computer is changing the way we work, think, learn, buy, and communicate. It's an opportunity to build a truly global village, and in the process of coming closer together, to reshape the ways of the world. But in order to do it we need to decommodify and democratize the new web order.

Periodical Bibliography

The following articles have been selected to supplement the diverse views presented in this chapter.

Ian Austen	"Meet the New Web, Same As the Old Web," *New York Times*, September 28, 2000.
Danny Bradbury	"Future Shock," *Computer Weekly*, May 10, 2001.
Marcel Bullinga	"The Internet of the Future," *Futurist*, May 2002.
Amir Dossal	"The UN in Action," *OECD Observer*, January 2001.
Peter F. Drucker	"Beyond the Information Revolution," *Atlantic Monthly*, October 1999.
Carter Henderson	"How the Internet Is Changing Our Lives," *Futurist*, July 2001.
Lawrence Lessig, interviewed by *Multinational Monitor*	"Controlling the 'Net," *Multinational Monitor*, March 2002.
Patrick Marshall	"Future of Computers," *CQ Researcher*, May 26, 2000.
Dwight D. Murphey	"Revolution on the Horizon," *St. Croix Review*, August 1998.
Raymond K. Neff	"Teleworld," *World & I*, May 2000.
Ian D. Pearson	"The Next Twenty Years in Technology: Timeline and Commentary," *Futurist*, January 2000.
Steven Pinker	"Life in the Fourth Millennium," *Technology Review*, May/June 2000.
Jennifer L. Schenker	"The Communications Revolution: A Brave New Web," *Time*, October 11, 1999.
Royal Van Horn	"Technology—What's Next?" *Phi Delta Kappan*, June 2000.
Chris Wood	"The Future: Will It Work?" *Maclean's*, August 21, 2000.

For Further Discussion

Chapter 1

1. In its viewpoint, Larry Irving maintains that the Information Revolution has created a digital divide. At the same time, he acknowledges that the number of minority households with access to information technology has increased significantly since the mid-1990s. Adam D. Thierer argues that personal computers and Internet access are now affordable for nearly all Americans. After considering the above information, and other arguments presented in the two viewpoints, please explain whether you believe the digital divide can be considered a serious and ongoing problem or if the gap is likely to become nonexistent in the coming years.

2. Robert J. Eaton is a former chairman of a major automobile company while Dwight R. Lee is a professor of economics. How do their respective jobs affect your opinion of the arguments they present concerning the economic role of the Internet?

3. Based on your personal experiences, do you believe that the Internet discourages social interactions, as purported by Andrew L. Shapiro, or do you support William J. Mitchell's assertion that the Internet encourages face-to-face interaction? Explain your answer.

Chapter 2

1. After reading the viewpoints in this chapter, what are your thoughts on the ways the Information Revolution has changed the American education system? Do you believe computers and Internet access are the cure-all for education or are there better, and perhaps less expensive, ways to improve schools? Explain your answer.

2. In their viewpoints on distance learning, both Kathleen B. Davey and Dave Wilson maintain that communication between students and teachers is essential to a quality education. Do you agree with their assertions? In addition, how do you think distance learning has affected the pupil-teacher relationship? Explain your answer.

3. William E. Kennard praises the federal E-Rate program in his viewpoint while Adam D. Thierer argues that state and local governments, not the federal government, should be responsible for funding education technologies. Whose argument do you find more convincing and why?

Chapter 3

1. Greg Miller argues that, despite the claims of the government and media, non-Internet companies pose a greater threat to the right to privacy than do websites. Assuming his argument is valid, why do you think that concerns about offline privacy are ignored, while coverage on the exploitation of personal data by Internet businesses is extensive? Explain your answer.

2. After reading the viewpoints by Theodore B. Olson and Mike Godwin, do you believe that community standards—which vary widely throughout the United States—are an effective way of determining whether online material is obscene? Why or why not?

3. In her viewpoint Bonnie J.K. Richardson contends that the Motion Picture Association of America is concerned about Internet piracy because it impedes digital trade. James Boyle asserts that the film industry has a history of overstating the dangers of new technologies. Which author do you believe offers a more accurate assessment of the effects of information technologies on copyrighted works and why?

Chapter 4

1. After reading the viewpoints in this chapter, how do you think the Information Revolution will change society? Do you believe that those changes will be largely positive or negative? Explain your answer.

2. In his viewpoint Kunda Dixit contends that developing nations should focus on improving health care and education rather than spend money on information technology. David Morrison maintains that technology will help impoverished nations increase the quality of their social services. Whose argument do you find more convincing and why?

3. Nicholas Imparato is a professor of marketing who emphasizes the competitive nature of the Information Revolution in his viewpoint. Andrew Hammer, a high-ranking official in two Socialist organizations, suggests that the Internet can help bring people together. After reading these perspectives, do you think that the Internet will unite communities or pit nations against each other? Do the authors' occupations affect your opinion? Explain your answers.

Organizations to Contact

The editors have compiled the following list of organizations concerned with the issues debated in this book. The descriptions are derived from materials provided by the organizations. All have publications or information available for interested readers. The list was compiled on the date of publication of the present volume; names, addresses, and phone numbers may change. Be aware that many organizations take several weeks or longer to respond to inquiries, so allow as much time as possible.

Berkman Center for Internet and Society
1587 Massachusetts Ave., Cambridge, MA 02138
(617) 495-7547 • fax: (617) 495-7641
e-mail: cyber@law.harvard.edu
website: http://cyber.harvard.edu

The Berkman Center for Internet and Society is a research organization whose members explore the challenges and opportunities of cyberspace. Its network of faculty, students, and affiliates research a number of Internet issues, among them intellectual property, privacy, and electronic commerce. Articles are available on its website, as are online seminars on issues like privacy and intellectual property.

Canada's Coalition for Public Information (CPI-CCIP)
200 Adelaide St. W., 3rd Fl., Toronto, ON, Canada M5H 1W7
(416) 977-6018 • fax: (416) 597-1617
e-mail: cpi@web.net
website: www.fis.utoronto.ca/people/affiliated/cpi

CPI-CCIP was founded in 1993 by the Ontario Library Association to ensure that the developing information infrastructure in Canada serves the public interest, focuses on human communication, and provides universal access to information. It is a coalition of organizations, public interest groups, and individuals that provides an effective grassroots voice for promoting and facilitating access to the benefits of telecomputing technology to maximize participation in a knowledge society and economy.

Center for Civic Networking (CCN)
PO Box 65272, Washington, DC 20037
(202) 362-3831 • fax: (202) 986-2539
e-mail: ccn-info@civicnet.org • website: www.civicnet.org

CCN is a nonprofit organization dedicated to applying information technology and infrastructure for the public good, particularly to improve access to information and the delivery of government services, to broaden citizen participation in government, and to stimulate economic and community development. It conducts policy research and analysis and consults with government and nonprofit organizations.

Center for Democracy and Technology (CDT)
1634 Eye St. NW, Suite 1100, Washington, DC 20006
(202) 637-9800 • fax: (202) 637-0968
e-mail: info@cdt.org • website: www.cdt.org

The mission of CDT is to develop public policy solutions that advance constitutional civil liberties and democratic values in new computer and communications media. Pursuing its mission through policy research, public education, and coalition building, the center works to increase citizens' privacy and the public's control over the use of personal information held by government and other institutions. Its publications include issue briefs, policy papers, and *CDT-Policy Posts*, an online, occasional publication that covers issues regarding the civil liberties of those using the information highway.

Center for Media Education (CME)
2120 L St. NW, Suite 200, Washington, DC 20037
(202) 331-7833
e-mail: cme@cme.org • website: www.cme.org

CME is a nonprofit public interest group concerned with media and telecommunications issues, such as educational television for children, universal public access to the information highway, and the development and ownership of information services. Its projects include the Campaign for Kids TV, which seeks to improve children's education; the Future of Media, concerning the information highway; and the Telecommunications Policy Roundtable of monthly meetings of nonprofit organizations. CME publications include articles on child online privacy and the digital divide, reports on online marketing and the marketing of tobacco and alcohol on the web, and fact sheets on Internet privacy.

Computing Research Association (CRA)
1875 Connecticut Ave. NW, Suite 718, Washington, DC 20009
(202) 234-2111 • fax: (202) 667-1066
e-mail: info@cra.org • website: http://cra.org

CRA seeks to strengthen research and education in the computing fields, expand opportunities for women and minorities, and educate the public and policy makers on the importance of computing research. CRA's publications include the bimonthly newsletter *Computing Research News.*

CyberAngels
Guardian Angels CyberAngels Program
PO Box 3009, Allentown, PA 18106
(610) 391-3012 • fax: (610) 391-3013
e-mail: caexec@cyberangels.org • website: www.cyberangels.org

CyberAngels helps law enforcement protect computer users—especially children—from stalkers and online predators. One of the organization's main objectives is to locate and report child pornography, which is illegal. CyberAngel's Net Patrol has helped law enforcement make arrests of online criminals.

Electronic Frontier Foundation (EFF)
454 Shotwell St., San Francisco, CA 94110-1914
(415) 436-9333 • fax: (415) 436-9993
e-mail: info@eff.org • website: www.eff.org

EFF is an organization of students and other individuals that aims to promote a better understanding of telecommunications issues. It fosters awareness of civil liberties issues arising from advancements in computer-based communications media and supports litigation to preserve, protect, and extend First Amendment rights in computing and telecommunications technologies. EFF provides information on topics such as encryption, cybersquatting, and Internet censorship and publishes the electronic newsletter *EFFector Online.*

Electronic Privacy Information Center (EPIC)
1718 Connecticut Ave. NW, Suite 200, Washington, DC 20009
(202) 483-1140 • fax: (202) 483-1248
e-mail: info@epic.org • website: www.epic.org

EPIC is an organization that advocates the public's right to electronic privacy. It sponsors educational and research programs, compiles statistics, and conducts litigation. Its publications include the biweekly electronic newsletter *EPIC Alert* and online reports.

International Society for Technology in Education (ISTE)
480 Charnelton St., Eugene, OR 97401-2626
(800) 336-5191 • (541) 302-3777 • fax: (541) 302-3778
e-mail: iste@iste.org • website: www.iste.org

ISTE is a multinational organization composed of teachers, administrators, and computer and curriculum coordinators. It facilitates the exchange of information and resources between international policy makers and professional organizations related to the fields of education and technology. The society also encourages research on and evaluation of the use of technology in education. It publishes the *Journal of Research on Technology in Education, Journal of Computing in Teacher Education, Learning & Leading with Technology*, and *Update* newsletter.

Internet Society

1775 Wiehle Ave., Suite 102, Reston, VA 20190-5108
(703) 326-9880 • fax: (703) 326-9881
e-mail: info@isoc.org • website: www.isoc.org

A group of technologists, developers, educators, researchers, government representatives, and businesspeople, the Internet Society supports the development and dissemination of standards for the Internet and works to ensure global cooperation and coordination for the Internet and related Internet-working technologies and applications. It publishes the bimonthly magazine *On the Internet.*

SafeSurf

3861-F North Main #256, Las Cruces, NM 88012
e-mail: safesurf@safesurf.com • website: www.safesurf.com

The goal of SafeSurf is to prevent children from accessing adult material—including pornography—on the Internet. It maintains that standards must be implemented on the Internet to protect children. SafeSurf reviews entertainment products such as children's computer games and awards a seal of excellence to exceptional products. The organization publishes the quarterly newsletter *SafeSurf News.*

Special Interest Group on Computers and Society (SIGCAS)

c/o Association for Computing Machinery
1515 Broadway, New York, NY 10036
(800) 342-6626 • (212) 626-0500 • fax: (212) 944-1318
e-mail: infodir_sigcas@acm.org • website: www.acm.org/sigcas

SIGCAS is composed of computer and physical scientists, professionals, and other individuals interested in issues concerning the effects of computers on society. It aims to inform the public of issues concerning computers and society through such publications as the quarterly newsletter *Computers and Society.*

Website

Global Internet Liberty Campaign (GILC)

e-mail: gilc@gilc.org • website: www.gilc.org

GILC is a coalition of civil liberties and human rights organizations, including the American Civil Liberties Union, the Electronic Privacy Information Center, Human Rights Watch, and the Internet Society, that seeks to reduce Internet censorship. The organization advocates against restrictive government and private controls over computer hardware and software and supports the right of online users to use encryption software. GILC publishes the newsletter *GILC Alert* and reports on topics such as filtering.

Bibliography of Books

Janet Abbate	*Inventing the Internet.* Cambridge, MA: MIT Press, 1999.
Alan B. Albarran and David H. Goff	*Understanding the Web: The Social, Political, and Economic Dimensions of the Internet.* Ames: Iowa State University Press, 2000.
Cynthia J. Alexander and Leslie A. Paul	*Digital Democracy: Policy and Politics in the Wired World.* New York: Oxford University Press, 1998.
Eric Banks	*E-Finance: The Electronic Revolution.* New York: John Riley & Sons, 2001.
David B. Bolt and Ray Crawford	*Digital Divide: Computers and Our Children's Future.* New York: TV Books, 2000.
Andrew Calcutt	*White Noise: An A–Z of the Contradictions in Cyberculture.* New York: St. Martin's Press, 1999.
Manuel Castells	*The Internet Galaxy: Reflections on the Internet, Business, and Society.* New York: Oxford University Press, 2001.
Center for Democracy and Technology	*Broadband Backgrounder: Public Policy Issues Raised by Broadband Technology.* www.cdt.org.
Michael Chesbro	*The Complete Guide to E-Security: Using the Internet and E-Mail Without Losing Your Privacy.* Boulder, CO: Paladin, 2000.
Benjamin Compaine	*The Digital Divide: Facing a Crisis or Creating a Myth.* Cambridge, MA: MIT Press, 2001.
James A. Dorn, ed.	*How the Internet Will Change the Economy.* Washington, DC: Cato Institute, 1999.
Jeanne M. Follman	*Getting the Web: Understanding the Nature and Meaning of the Internet.* Chicago: Duomo Press, 2001.
Simson Garfinkel	*Database Nation: The Death of Privacy in the 21st Century.* Cambridge, MA: O'Reilly & Associates, 2001.
Global Internet Liberty Campaign	*Regardless of Frontiers: Protecting the Human Right to Freedom of Expression on the Global Internet.* www.gilc.org/speech/report.
Mike Godwin	*Cyber Rights: Defending Free Speech in the Digital Age.* New York: Random House, 1998.
Edward E. Hindson and Lee Frederickson	*Future Wave: End Times, Prophecy, and the Technological Explosion.* Eugene, OR: Harvest House, 2001.

Joshua Migga Kizza

Civilizing the Internet: Global Concerns and Efforts Toward Regulation. Jefferson, NC: McFarland, 1998.

Alex Lightman

Brave New Unwired World: The Digital Big Bang and the Infinite Internet. New York: John Wiley & Sons, 2002.

Robert E. Litan and Alice M. Rivlin, eds.

The Economic Payoff from the Internet Revolution. Washington, DC: Brookings Institution Press, 2001.

William J. Mitchell

E-Topia. Cambridge, MA: MIT Press, 2000.

Christos J.P. Moschovitis

History of the Internet: A Chronology, 1843 to the Present. Santa Barbara, CA: ABC-CLIO, 1999.

John Naughton

A Brief History of the Future: Origins of the Internet. New York: Overlook Press, 2000.

Alan L. Porter and William H. Read

The Information Revolution: Current and Future Consequences. Westport, CT: Greenwood, 1998.

Gene I. Rochlin

Trapped in the Net: The Unanticipated Consequences of Computerization. New Jersey: Princeton University Press, 1998.

Dan Schiller

Digital Capitalism: Networking the Global Market System. Cambridge, MA: MIT Press, 1999.

Andrew L. Shapiro

The Control Revolution: How the Internet Is Putting Individuals in Charge and Changing the World We Know. New York: PublicAffairs, 1999.

Mark J. Stefik

The Internet Edge: Social, Technological, and Legal Challenges for a Networked World. Cambridge, MA: MIT Press, 1999.

Clifford Stoll

High Tech Heretic: Reflections of a Computer Contrarian. New York: Anchor Press, 2000.

Patricia M. Wallace

The Psychology of the Internet. New York: Cambridge University Press, 1999.

Gary Young, ed.

The Internet. New York: H.W. Wilson, 1998.

Index

Abdullah II (king of Jordan), 168
age factors in access to information technology, 26
Algebra Tutor, 75
American Civil Liberties Union (ACLU), 121–22
American Civil Liberties Union v. Reno, 127
American Memory Fellows program, 72–73
America Online, 19
Annenberg Foundation, 85
Anti-Defamation League, 19–20
Astronomy Digital Image Library, 72
Athena computer network, 54–55
automobile industry, 40–42

Bangladesh, 169–70, 174
Berne Convention, 139
Boucher, Rick, 14–15
Boyle, James, 141
Brandeis, Louis, 109
broadcast video, 85
Brown, Stacia, 19
Burns, Conrad R., 115
Bush, George W., 99, 100
businesses and economy
  efficiency of operations with, 155
  free or subsidized PCs to employees in, 35
  future of Internet shopping and, 154–55
  impact of computers on, 14–15
  information technology and
    Internet's impact on, 16, 42–43, 164
    automobile industry and, 40–42
    as changing everything, 39–40
      con, 45
    developing nations and, 169–70
    economic benefits and, 41
    improving market communication and, 46–47
    productivity and, 42
    role of market prices vs., 45–46
  New Economy and, 39
  obscenity and, 128–30
  wearable computers and, 151
  see also entertainment and computer industries

cable systems, 35
California Virtual Campus, 92
campaigns, online, 182–83
Carnegie Learning, 75
Carnivore/DCS1000, 104

Carson, Rachel, 112
Castells, Manuel, 51
Center for Children and Technology, 72
Centre for Energy and Climate Solutions (CECS), 162
Challenge Grant Program, 76
Chaney, Helen, 35
Child Online Protection Act (1998)
  background of, 121
  community standards and, 122–24, 127
  is challenged, 121–22
  legal limits in, 131, 133
  narrow focus of, 130–31
civil rights. *See* privacy rights
Clark, Jim, 39
Clinton administration, 32, 33
Coates, Joseph F., 152
Cohen, Eric, 32
Communications Decency Act (CDA), 133
community. *See* social interaction
compressed video systems, 87
computer industry. *See* entertainment and computer industries
computers
  decreasing costs of, 33
  demographics of access to, 26–27
  effect of, on business, 16
  free services for, 34–35
  giving away, 33, 42
  increased access to, 22–23
  languages and, 157–58
  level of education as impacting access to, 25, 29
"cookies," 117–18
Copenhaver, Brian P., 92
Copyright Clause, 143–44
copyright theft, 135–36
  problems with jurisdiction on, 137–39
Corporation for Public Broadcasting, 85
correspondence courses, 85, 90
Council on Competitiveness, 178
Court, Randolph, 117
cyber-unions, 155–56

Davey, Kathleen B., 83
Dertouzos, Michael, 50, 161
developing nations
  information technology as improving, 167–70
    con, 166–67

Internet as a tool for mobilization in, 170–71
Internet usage in, 168, 174–75
radio vs. Internet use in, 176
technology is not a cure-all for, 173–74
Diagnostic Reading Assessment, 75
digital archives, 72
digital divide, 15
on access to Internet, 23–24, 27–28
on computer ownership, 15, 22, 23
decreasing costs and, 33–35
demographic factors and, 26–27
between developed and developing countries, 173–74, 184
divide in educational skills vs., 36–37
future of, 163–64
government steps to solve, 32–33
government subsidy programs would not help, 36
growth of, 22, 27–28
harm of subsidies for, 34
household type as factor in, 25–26
income factor in, 23–24, 29
level of education as factor in, 25, 29
as likely to continue, 29–30
racial/ethnic origin factor in, 24–25, 28–29
see also developing nations; E-Rate program
Digital Millennium Copyright Act, 136
Digital Opportunities Task Force (DOT Force), 166
digital subscriber line (DSL), 35
distance learning, 84
challenges to, 86–87
development of, 84–86
economic motivations for, 91–92
educational technology has benefited, 87–88
key claims on, 84
loss of connection with instructor through, 90–91
quality of education is not guaranteed with, 91
student-teacher relationship is lacking in, 92
as supplanting campus-based learning, 88
con, 90
Dixit, Kunda, 172
dot.com businesses, 16
DSC1000 (Carnivore), 104
dumb terminals, 35
Dyson, Esther, 64

Eaton, Robert J., 38

e-commerce, 40
Economist (magazine), 160, 173
economy. *See* businesses and economy
educational technology
ability to afford, 79–80
business partnership with schools for, 80–81
digital archives and, 72
digital divide and, 25, 29
factors needed for effectiveness of, 74–75
improved teacher instruction with, 71–72
increased parental involvement with, 82
Internet plagiarism in, 68–69
Internet's impact on, 15–16
is not effectively used, 81–82
positive effects of, 71
possibilities in, 76–77
role of federal government in, 75–76
should be prioritized over Internet in developing nations, 176
students expressing their ideas through, 73–74
teacher collaboration with, 72–73
United States as unprepared for, 179
will not replace critical thinking, 82
see also distance learning; higher education
Education and Library Networks Coalition (EdLINC), 95
education rate program. *See* E-Rate program
e-mail, 34, 104
entertainment and computer industries
digital delivery of content by, 135
as needing government support, 139–40
preventing copyright theft in, 135–37
see also intellectual property protection and rights
environmental crisis, 108–109
Equifax, 107, 110
E-Rate program, 76
does not help poor libraries, 100
ending federal involvement in, 100–101
funding for, 99–100
increased Internet access with, 96
public support for, 95
success of, 94–95, 96–97
teacher effectiveness with technology and, 96–97
as unnecessary, 99
Expert Technology Panel, 76

Falling Through the Net (NTIA report), 15, 22
Federal Bureau of Investigation (FBI), 104
Federal Communications Commission (FCC), 96, 99–100
federal education programs. *See* E-Rate program
Federal Trade Commission (FTC), 115
filtering programs, 19–20
Ford Motor Company, 42
Forrester Research, 33
Free Burma Coalition, 183

G8 summit (Okinawa), 166
Gambia, 169
Garfinkel, Simson, 106
Gates, Bill, 166, 173
gender differences, 184
Gentry, Dennis, 53
Georgetown University, 115
Ginsberg v. New York (1968), 127
Gibson, William, 53
Givens, Beth, 114–15
Global Positioning Satellite system (GPS), 158
Godin, Seth, 118–19
Godwin, Mike, 120
Golrick, Michael, 100
Gore, Al, 14, 79, 99
government
    lack of funding for information and technology by, 179
    must protect privacy rights, 110–11
    surveillance of e-mails by, 104
    see also E-Rate program
Grameen Phone (Bangladesh), 169–70
Groupware, 155

Hague Convention, 137–39
Hambrecht, William, 178
Hamline v. United States (1974), 129–30
Hammer, Andrew, 181
handheld PC devices, 35
HateFilter, 19–20
Hendricks, Evan, 111
Hickman, John N., 68, 69
higher education
    independent study courses/programs for, 85
    location of Internet availability in, 55–56
    telecourses for, 85–86
    see also distance learning
Holmes, Maurice, 179–80
homeless population, 49

HomeNet study, 64–65
home video playback, 85
Honey, Margaret, 70
Horn, Stacy, 54
hybrid computing systems, 35

Imparato, Nicholas, 177
independent study courses/programs, 85
India, 173–74, 178
information technology
    America's competition with other countries in, 178–79
    impact of, on the economy, 16
    as improving teacher instruction, 71–72
    predictions on, 14–15
    United States should learn new technologies in, 179–80
    see also computers; Internet
Intel, 118
intellectual property protection and rights
    argument for, 143–44
    con, 144–45
    changing nature of public domain and, 146
    copyright and, 135–39
    economics of, 145–46
    expansion on, 142–43
    videotapes and, 146–47
    see also entertainment and computer industries
Internet
    accessibility of ideas on, 182–83
    access to, 23–24, 29, 35
    connecting developing nations to, 168
    democratic features of, 153
    demographics of access to, 26–27
    energy consumption from, 162–63
    family composition influencing access to, 26
    free or cheap access to, 34
    future of
        building democracy and, 183
        cannot benefit developing nations, 166–67
        efficient business operations and, 155
        increasing safety in, 157
        interorganizational negotiations and, 156–57
        language used in, 157–58
        major changes in, 153–54
        medicine and, 158
        reducing inequality in, 164
        shopping and, 154–55

sightseeing and, 158
as transforming the home, 158–59
will not end wars, 161–62
will not solve environmental
    problems, 162
gender differences on use of, 184
impact of, on education, 15–16
level of education as impacting access
    to, 25, 29
media professional employment for,
    156
need to democratize, 185–86
percentage of schools connected to,
    79
plagiarism with, 68–69
proper use of, 175–76
racial/ethnic factors in access to,
    24–25, 28–29
replaces face-to-face communication,
    184–85
statistics on world usage of, 174, 175
wireless, 35, 153–54, 158
see also computers; information
    technology; obscenity; privacy
    rights; social interaction, on the
    Internet
Internet cafes, 55
Internet service providers (ISPs), 19
Ireland, 178
Irving, Larry, 21

Jackson, Jesse, 33
Jenkins v. Georgia (1974), 132–33
Jordan, 168
Jubilee 2000 campaign, 183

Kennard, William E., 93
Kosko, Bart, 104

labor unions, 155–56
language, 157–58
Lee, Dwight R., 44
LeFevre, Andrew T., 78
legislation
    on computer security, 111
    on copyright theft, 136–37
    see also Child Online Protection Act;
        intellectual property protection and
        rights; Telecommunications Act
libraries, 100
Library of Congress, 72–73
Lotus, 110
Louis Harris & Associates, 107
Louvre Museum, 72

Mahajan, Pramod, 173–74
Man, John, 157–58
Marockie, Hank, 97

Massachusetts Institute of Technology
    (MIT), 161
Matzorkis, Nick, 116
media, 59–60
medicine, 158
Meisner, Karen, 53
Metrocard system, 107–108
Mfume, Kweisi, 33
Microsoft, 118
Miller, Greg, 113
Miller v. California (1973), 121–22, 127
minorities, 28
Mitchell, William J., 48
mobile telephones, 169–70
Morrison, David, 165
Motion Picture Association of America
    (MPAA), 135
MP3, 145–46

National Alliance, 19
National Center for Education
    Statistics, 79
National Center for Supercomputing,
    72
National Education Association
    (NEA), 15
National Science Foundation, 76
National Telecommunications and
    Information Administration (NTIA),
    15, 21, 22
Negroponte, Nicholas, 60, 161
Nepal, 173, 174
New Economy, 39, 40
Noble, David F., 90

obscenity
    can be regulated in public spaces
        only, 124–25
    community standards on, 121–22,
        127–28
        are reasonably constant, 132
    should be regulated, 125
off-campus education. See distance
    learning
Office of Educational Technology, 75
Office of Technology Assessment
    (OTA), 112
official development assistance (ODA),
    167
Old Economy, 43
Olson, Theodore B., 126
online campaigns, 182–83
Online Privacy Alliance, 115

Palm Pilots, 71–72
paper mills, 68
patent laws, 142–43
patents, 178

PC Data Incorporated, 33
PCs (personal computers). *See* computers
Peruvian Ministry of Health, 170
Pitofsky, Robert, 118
plagiarism, Internet, 68–69
Pope v. Illinois (1987), 131
pornography. *See* obscenity
poverty. *See* developing nations; digital divide
privacy rights
  consumer backlash and awareness of, 118–19
  "cookies" and, 117–18
  government must protect, 110–11
  government surveillance of e-mails and, 104–105
  guarding off-line violations of, 115–16
  identity theft and, 118
  individual actions to prevent, 110
  Metrocard system and, 107–108
  need for legislation on computer security for, 111–12
  need for published reports on, 112
  off-line threats to privacy vs. threats to, 114–15
  surveys on, 107
  threatened through Internet, 107
  as an unnecessary trade-off for technology, 108–10
  website privacy policies and, 114, 115
Privacy Rights Clearinghouse, 114
public domain, 146
Public Electronic Network (PEN), 49
Putnam, Robert, 61

race/ethnic origin, 28–29
radio, 176
Rheingold, Howard, 53–54
Richardson, Bonnie J.K., 134
Riley, Richard W., 14
Roszak, Theodore, 62
Rotenberg, Marc, 115–16
Roth v. United States (1957), 127, 128

Sable Communications, Inc. v. FCC (1989), 129–30
Saffo, Paul, 16
Santa Fe Science and Technology, 151
Schwartz, David, 117–18
Segovia, Roy, 116
Shapiro, Andrew L., 57
Shatnawi, Saleh, 118
Shaw, David, 180
shopping, Internet, 154–55
Shostak, Arthur, 155

Silent Spring (Carson), 112
social interaction
  history of community, 58
  on the Internet
    anonymity with, 49
    as a danger to communities, 62–63
    as a distraction from local and physical world, 64
    fluidity of relationships with, 63–64
    as fostering human contact, 53
    globalizing effect of, 51–52
    increases desire for face-to-face interaction, 52–54
      con, 184–85
    increases isolation and depression, 64–65
    through locations of connection, 54–56
    narrow view of life through, 60–62
    safety with, 49
    as widening tertiary social circles, 50–51
  mass media and, 59–60
  sharing information/experiences and, 58–59
Social Security Administration, 110
software
  benefits education, 71
  educational, 75
  filtering, 19–20
Sonny Bono Term Extension Act, 145
South Asia, 174
South Korea, 178
spam, 118
Sri Lanka, 174
Stevens, John Paul, 124
Stormfront, 19

Taiwan, 178
Telecommunications Act (1996), 96, 99
telecourses, 85
telephones, mobile, 169–70
television costs, 33–34
terrorists, e-mails of, 104
Thierer, Adam D., 31, 98
ThinkQuest, 74
Third Circuit Court of Appeals, 121–23, 128, 130
third-world nations. *See* developing nations
Trade-Related Aspects of Intellectual Property Rights (TRIPS), 139

United Nations Development Programme (UNDP), 168
United States
  Department of Education, 75
  information technology challenges

in, 178–79
military, 150
should learn new technologies,
179–80
Universal Service Administration
Company (USAC), 99
universities. *See* higher education

Valenti, Jack, 135
van Opstal, Debra, 178
Varney, Christine, 115
video piracy, 135–36
video recorders, 146–47
video systems, interactive, 87
Voxiva, 170

Warren, Samuel, 109
Watson, Thomas J., 14
wearable computers, 150
websites
automobile industry and, 40–41

personal information collected by,
109
privacy policies on, 107, 114, 115
racist and hate-filled, 19–20
selling research papers and essays on,
68
Weiss, Peter, 150
Well, the, 53–54
Wenglinsky, Harold, 81
Western Governors University
(WGN), 91–92
Wilson, Dave, 89
Winzel, Pär, 53
Wireless Generation, 71, 75
wireless telecommunications, 153–54
World Bank, 167, 168
World Church of the Creator
(WCOTC), 19
World Intellectual Property
Organization (WIPO), 136